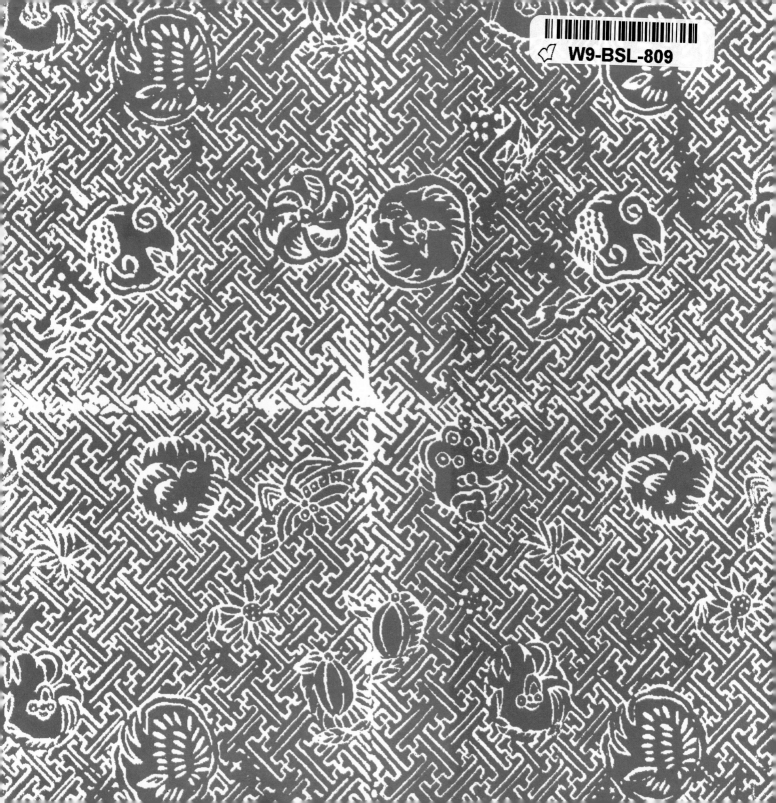

Tea with Miss Rose

Tea with Miss Rose

Recipes & Reminiscences
of Boston's Teacup Society

by Elizabeth Driscoll and
Elaine Negroponte

with an essay by Belinda Rathbone

Published by Mount Vernon Press
Boston, Massachusetts

Printer: South China Printing Company Limited, Hong Kong

Endpapers: Tea paper pattern taken from Dr. Nichols' study at the Nichols House Museum

ISBN 0-9721155-0-1

Acknowledgments
Many people have helped us with this book, and we are indeed grateful to all of them. A very special thanks to our editors, Maria Capello and Ellen Hoffman; Nicholas Negroponte for his encouragement; Dimitri Negroponte for his technical advice and assistance; Frederick Brink for his help with technical graphics; Elise Brink for her research assistance and support; and the Driscoll family for their support and encouragement.

The authors also wish to thank Mary Thomsen for her skill at testing the recipes included in this volume, Betsy Chimento for graphic design assistance, Gail Weesner for copy editing, Fritz Westman for creating the Suggested Tour map, Paul Leahy for his drawings, Flavia Cigliano and John Sutherland for encouragement, Joan and Charles Platt for generously giving us their Cornish recipes, Joan and William Shurcliff, and Polly Thayer Starr for graciously sharing memories, William H. Pear II for his extensive knowledge of the Nichols family, Constance V. R. White for providing the "missing recipe," Mary Bicknell at the Massachusetts State House Special Collections, Sally Hinkle for recipe testing, Evelyn Farnum, Patricia Sullivan, Gail Banks, and finally James Borden for his day-to-day help.

To the Reader

The idea for a book on teas first took shape when I was asked to give a formal tea party. I found a paucity of material on how to organize a proper tea party, and soon realized that more misinformation was available than reliable advice on how to entertain in this traditional way. My intention took a more interesting turn when co-author Elizabeth Driscoll added a cache of recipes by Mary King, cook and housekeeper to Rose Standish Nichols, an eminent Boston lady. These recipes, along with author Belinda Rathbone's essay, gave us the opportunity to draw a portrait of Miss Nichols, an important but largely unknown garden historian and landscape architect. The end result is a soupçon of Boston history, period recipes, a "how to" section on preparing a tea, and a suggested walking tour of places of interest touched upon in this book.

As I look around Beacon Hill today, I find myself thankful to Rose Nichols for her foresight and determination in preserving her Mount Vernon Street home. Through the condominium conversions of the 1980s, and then a reversal back to single-family dwellings in the 1990s, both prosperity and youthful vitality arrived in full force to redo most of the interiors of the houses on the Hill. We are indeed fortunate to have been left this one historic house, kept as it was during Miss Nichols' lifetime, which offers an invaluable and enduring sense of a disappearing past.

In this spirit, *Tea with Miss Rose* attempts to capture a little of the tenor of Rose Nichols' Boston. Rather than a complete work on tea, a lesson in Boston history, or a biography, it is more like an afternoon's visit to 55 Mount Vernon Street—a glimpse into a period when Bostonians helped to define the art of the formal tea party.

We hope that you might find enough inspiration in these pages to try your hand at this delightful culinary art form. For while some contend that formal tea parties belong to older, more conventional days, it has been said—and we believe—that "when too many conventions disappear, a certain grace goes with them."

E.N.

Preface

The climate of Boston and the temperament of its people did not easily lend itself to the leisured pace of a *café society*, which flourished in cities such as Paris or Barcelona in the early 1900s. Instead, Boston's *Brahmins*—the name coined by Oliver Wendell Holmes to describe that special breed of upper-class Yankee men and women—found that a *Teacup Society* better suited them in every way. The men and women of Boston's institutions of culture and learning offered an abundance of opinions to keep conversation lively, and the tea party provided the perfect transport to display such talent. Make no mistake, however, in thinking that the tea party was for pleasure alone. In Boston, in particular, it was put to good use by ladies to further any number of social and political agendas at a time when few other means were available to them.

While our protagonist, Rose Standish Nichols, promoted world peace at her tea parties, other ladies waged their own campaigns using "tea and petits fours."

The first Audubon Society began in Boston, it is said, over tea, "one cup at a time," when in 1896, Boston blueblood Mrs. Harriet Lawrence Hemenway read about the great carnage of some five million birds, in part due to the rage for plumed hats. With newspaper article in hand, she trotted across Clarendon Street to her cousin Minna Hall. "There, over tea, they plotted their strategy to put a halt to the cruel slaughter. Taking *The Boston Blue Book* down from a shelf, they ticked off the names of Brahmin ladies most likely to wear feathers, and proceeded to plan a series of teas." It was over cups of hot Hu-Kwa and delicate pastries that Harriet and Minna formed a group of women, 900 strong, to protect our native birds from becoming plumage for fashion. They named their group the Massachusetts Audubon Society after the great bird painter, John James Audubon.

Over time the activist ladies of Boston's Beacon Hill and Back Bay —the essence of the *Teacup Society*—if not destined for extinction, would see their numbers diminish. But not before they, along with the women in their service who prepared and served the teas, had created a legacy of distinction—more often than not over a bracing cup of China tea.

Contents

Rose Standish Nichols
August 1953

Part One

Rose Standish Nichols: A Portrait

by Belinda Rathbone

Beacon Hill

Rose Standish Nichols, celebrated as the first female landscape architect in America, was in fact a woman of many mediums. She not only designed gardens, but wrote extensively on garden design and garden history. She also designed interiors, and to that end became an accomplished needleworker and woodcarver. By the time she retired from professional life in the 1950s and returned from her travels to live full time at the family home on Boston's Beacon Hill, she had acquired a rich transcontinental network of friends and acquaintances. She was fluent in world politics, European nobility, American society, art and architecture, theater, music, and literature. In short, she was as broadly educated as any lady of her generation.

Now everything else Rose Nichols had achieved in her life served to create the stage, the players, and the plot for what was her personal theater: the afternoon tea party. She infused these soirees with the sophistication and sense of history she had acquired over thirty years of travel abroad, and most of all with her insatiable appetite for bringing people together and making them fizz.

Tea with Rose Nichols was really a salon. These gatherings had a purpose, and it was not to discuss the weather. "The whole point of these teas was not really tea but to get people of different beliefs together," recalled her nephew's wife, who was frequently asked "to pour." Rose Nichols believed that challenging their beliefs led her guests to find the common ground on which all people stand and make peace with each other. She would invite an arch conservative, like William Loeb, editor of the *Manchester Union Leader*, with a nice young Harvard student who happened to be a communist, and sort of steer them toward each other, "because she thought they ought to argue together, and they did too!"

One Beacon Hill neighbor and frequent tea guest, the poet Frances Howard, confessed, "I was never really sure why she asked me; we disagreed on every conceivable subject." But that was exactly what interested Rose. It was not the combination of ginger with cloves that concerned her (that was the cook, Mary King's department) but rather a dash of liberal and a pinch of conservative that promised a good tea. Controversy was her spice.

Should you have been among the carefully chosen twelve or fifteen people of divergent views to appear at number 55 Mount Vernon Street on a Sunday afternoon, you would make your way from the front hall up the circular staircase to the dining room, with its family portraits set against dark floral wallpaper resembling embossed leather. The large mahogany table was laid with trays of tea sandwiches, cakes, and cookies. One of the lady guests would be asked to pour—an honor, though a dubious one, as she would be lucky to get a cup of tea herself before the supply ran completely dry. Meanwhile the other guests had plenty of time to graze and mingle and gently warm up to the conversational challenges that lay ahead.

Presiding over her gatherings, Rose Nichols had a stately presence, the *saloniste* par excellence. She was tall, lean, and theatrically dressed—favoring dark velvets and embroidered bodices which, like her garden designs, hinted at Medieval and Renaissance origins. She always wore a hat, and her hats "were like velvet puddings" as the artist Polly Thayer recalled, anchored firmly by her long thin face, sidelong glance, and arched brow. Rose herself was known to have never eaten a thing at her own parties. She declared that she could not talk and eat at the same time, and given the choice, she would always choose to talk. For Rose, "nourishment was of the mind," as Mary King wryly observed.

From the dining room Rose directed the party across the hall to the drawing room, upon which she had lavished her eclectic taste for Medieval Flemish tapestry, English furniture, Japanese porcelain, and Persian carpets, blended here in an overall color scheme probably best described as Old Rose, which now the late afternoon sun bathed in a spray of gold. Here the guests would seat themselves to form a circle. In her distinctive low voice, which some would describe as lugubrious, Rose would call on someone in the group. "Mr. Mitchell! I understand you've just returned from China. Can you tell us about it?"

"She would pick on people who would be loud and interesting," recalled her nephew. "Maybe after twenty minutes or so she would shoot to a new topic. She expressed not the slightest interest in jokes, or small talk or the weather." Frances Howard, a frequent guest, recalled that if the party was suitably conservative Rose "would throw out some remark like, 'I feel we have been unreasonably rude to the poor dear Russians.' She would then sit back and bask in the fireworks." In the absence of a hot political issue, she would throw out some sprawling topic like, "What is your idea of heaven?"

Emerging somewhat later (on a particularly lively evening, as late as eight o'clock), with increasing gratitude for Mary King's cakes and tea sandwiches and your mental faculties quite exhausted, you would have had to admit that something had happened. You had met someone you might otherwise have assiduously avoided. A stranger had become a friend. You had mixed with the younger, or the older generation. You had warmed to a foreigner, a commoner, or a nobleman, and forgotten the difference. Your fondly held opinions had been tickled or teased or simply trashed. You had participated in what Rose Nichols considered to be that great Puritan tradition: the broadening of the mind.

Born in Boston in 1872, Rose Standish Nichols was the eldest of the three daughters of Dr. Arthur Nichols, a physician, and

Elizabeth Fisher Homer. Both of staunch New England stock, they took pride in their legacy of good breeding and good health. Dr. Nichols observed that his relations were "characterized by their large frame and sound constitution, and were remarkably free from tuberculosis, cancer, insanity, and other hereditary disorders." They were also fortunate to have some inherited wealth.

The family moved from Roxbury Highlands to the house at 55 Mount Vernon Street in 1885. The house was allegedly designed by Charles Bulfinch, but whether it was or not, its circular staircase (adding elegance and intrigue to the entrance hall), the attractive proportions of its rooms, and its commanding position at the crest of Beacon Hill (looking down the hill towards the river rather than across the street at its neighbors), combined to make it an important looking house. To grow up in this house, as Rose did from the age of thirteen, was to live up to it, and Rose was determined to do so in every way.

At a young age, Rose started to take a leading role in family affairs, dominating her younger sisters Marian and Margaret, conferring with her father in the matters of the house and garden, and enhancing her mother's social life. In the 1890s Rose founded the Beacon Hill Reading Club, not only for her own enjoyment but with her mother in mind, believing that the older should mix with the younger generation on the Hill. They met weekly all winter long, each member taking a turn at hosting the group, selecting and reading the text, and then leading a discussion afterward. Thus Rose Nichols began her career in the art of conversation

*Saint-Gaudens (third from left)
and family, with tea on the
piazza in Cornish, circa 1898.
(Courtesy of the State Library of
Massachusetts)*

among the well-read ladies of Boston, an experience among many others that would form the foundations of her famous Sunday afternoons.

Cornish

In the 1880s the Nichols family rented a summer house in Rye Beach, New Hampshire. It was Rose, aged eighteen, who persuaded her family to move from there inland to Cornish, a dwindling farm community, in 1892. The move was inspired by Augustus Saint-Gaudens, celebrated sculptor of monuments and memorials in New York and Boston, who was also Rose's uncle by marriage. The Nichols family had spent part of the summer of 1889 in the old brick roadhouse near Blow-Me-Down Creek which Saint-Gaudens and his wife Augusta (thus Uncle Gus and Aunt Gussie to the Nichols girls) had bought in Cornish in 1885. They had transformed the once bleak and tumbledown house into an airy interior with a colonnaded porch and terraced gardens, and renamed it "Aspet" after the Saint-Gaudens' ancestral home in France.

At the turn of the century Cornish was a burgeoning artists' colony. At Saint-Gaudens' urging, artists of every kind—sculptors, painters, and illustrators such as Daniel Chester French, Frances Grimes, Maxfield Parrish, Everett Shinn, Kenyon Cox, and

Thomas and Maria Oakley Dewing, as well as writers and editors Winston Churchill (a distant cousin of the statesman), Herbert Croly, and Maxwell Perkins, the actress Ethel Barrymore, and the three singing Fuller Sisters—converged there from New York and Boston to escape the summer heat and to work. Unlike Newport or Bar Harbor, where the rich decamped for the sea breeze and high society, Cornish—high in the Green Mountains of New Hampshire—was the setting for "an aristocracy of brains," as a New York journalist coined it, a haven for those in search of stimulating company along with an informal life in a wild and beautiful landscape.

"My artistic sister Rose," recalled Margaret Nichols, the youngest of the three, "set her heart on our buying a place in Cornish. I had very little enthusiasm for faraway Cornish, with no marsh, no ocean, and no friends." But these features mattered less to Rose than the enlightened company of her elder luminaries. As usual, noted Margaret, "Rose had her way."

In 1891 the Nichols family bought the Chester Pike Farm, with a large though undistinguished house, a couple of barns, and one hundred and fifty acres of land just down the hill from Uncle Gus. They renamed the farm "Mastlands," because of the tall fir trees on the property, which were once harvested to make ship's masts. Before long Rose was planning improvements to the house and the garden that would be up to the standards of their artistic Cornish neighbors.

Among the brains of Cornish was Charles Platt, the well-known New York architect, who was Rose's first tutor in the principles of design. Platt, who had begun his career as an artist, was inspired in Cornish to take up architecture and garden design, and designed many of the gardens that were to become the pride of the Cornish colonists. He conceived of the garden as an extension of the house, as "an outdoor living room"; his signature style combined the architectural formality of the Italian Renaissance garden with the floral abundance of the English cottage garden.

Eager to apply her lessons to practice, Rose created her first garden out of the farmyard at Mastlands. Surrounded by a brick wall, the Nichols' outdoor living room radiated from a central axis in line with the house into smaller subsidiary axes. In its planting scheme Rose attended to the contrast of vertical and horizontal, of light- with dark-leafed shrubs, of feathery with hard, softening the formality of the layout with rangy and abundant flower beds of pink cosmos, blue larkspur, and heliotrope. She preserved an old apple tree as the centerpiece of the garden, and built a small decorative pool for it to reflect in. At the end of the garden she placed a bench, above which she framed the distant view of majestic Mount Ascutney. The result, as her friend and fellow colonist Frances Duncan described it, was "the ideal garden of a house in the country . . . not an exhibition grounds, nor even a flower show, but a lovable place where one is inclined to lounge or read in undisturbed peace."

The gardens of Cornish were as much for society as for undisturbed peace, and the Nichols garden was no exception. Colonists worked hard by day at their painting or poetry; by sunset they were eager to mingle in one another's stimulating company. Afternoons and evenings were spent sharing drinks, picnics, conversation, musicales, theatricals, and games of charades. Gardens were often the settings for these gatherings, white or bright colors were the recommended dress code for women, and tea was often the drink. In the absence of an invitation to tea, the Cornish colonists might find each other at The Tea Tray, the popular tea house on route 12A, for which Maxfield Parrish painted a charming double-sided sign.

There were other opportunities and reasons to gather in Cornish. Rose joined the Cornish Women's Suffrage League in 1911. She was also a founding member two years later of the Cornish Discussion Club, a group of ladies that included Lydia (Mrs. Maxfield) Parrish, Mabel (Mrs. Winston) Churchill, and Ellen (Mrs. Woodrow) Wilson. The ladies would boldly delve into such sweeping questions as "Does human nature change?" or "What constitutes a good citizen?" or "The simple life: what is it and is it worthwhile?" During the First World War this group evolved into the more activist League of Small Nations to discuss the plight of smaller countries such as Finland.

Rose's approach was always global, to think large as well as small, to appreciate potential as much as power. "What matters to me," she once said, "is not what a person is, but what he or she would like to be." Lydia Parrish described Rose's way of talking about people as simply "gossip on a very high plane."

As a young woman Rose was determined to develop her career in landscape design. In 1891, Uncle Gus invited his favorite niece to live with them in New York where she learned to draw at the Art Students League and apprenticed in the architectural offices of Thomas Hastings. After one year in New York, Rose returned to Boston and continued her architectural studies at MIT as a "special student," as she was the only female.

Through Platt and Saint-Gaudens, Rose Nichols rapidly developed an impressive list of American clients. Her first assignment in Newport, Rhode Island, for Ellen Mason led to many others. The grandest suburban communities beckoned her (Tuxedo Park, New York; Lake Forest, Illinois), as well as summer retreats (Pittsfield, Massachusetts) and winter resorts (Tucson, Arizona; Santa Barbara, California). No matter where she practiced, whether in the Berkshire hills or the Southwestern desert, Rose Nichols' training in architecture had provided her with a strong background in layout and form. Charles Platt's preference for the formal over the romantic school of landscape design, a subject hotly debated among designers at the time, influenced Rose from the start and remained a constant principle throughout her career.

Marian (left) and Rose (right)
with a friend in Salzburg,
July 1894

Europe

It was first her schooling and later her scholarship that led Rose to spend as much as half her life in Europe. After New York and Boston, she continued to refine her eye and enlarge her knowledge abroad, first in Paris, attending the Ecole des Beaux Arts, and later in London at the Courtauld Institute. From the Sesame Club in West London, where she would install herself for a stretch of several months, her letters home to her mother and sisters would report a hectic social life of teas ("with various countesses"), musicales, dinners, opera, and theater. Seizing every opportunity for enlightened conversation she observed that "Englishmen are much more interesting than the average American men, though I think the girls at home are ahead of those here."

In her introduction to *English Pleasure Gardens*, her first book, Rose makes clear her preference for the French and Italian styles, virtually dismissing the designed landscape for which England was so famous as "eighteenth century extremes." She focused her particular attention on those gardens that had escaped the sweeping changes of Lancelot "Capability" Brown, and where the formalities of the Renaissance could still be seen, such as those of Longleat, Wilton, Bowood, and Penshurst. She usually succeeded in winning a private tour of the garden by the head gardener if not the titled owner himself. As the American lady abroad, she would repay her many social debts with an invitation to join her for tea at the Sesame Club.

From her London post, Rose followed with intense interest her Uncle Augustus' latest triumphs, and with her mother, joined Saint-Gaudens in Paris on the occasion of the unveiling of the plaster cast of his monument to General Sherman in April 1900. Larger than life, Sherman rides behind a handsome angel of victory. "It's the grandest victory anyone ever made," Saint-Gaudens boasted to his niece, and the whole family took pride in its central position under the skylit dome of the Grand Palais.

Above all, Rose Nichols' agenda in Europe was to study gardens and garden history, not just for the sake of her commissions in America, but as material for her magazine articles in *The Century* (whose editor, Willa Cather, would become a lifelong friend and correspondent), *The House Beautiful,* and especially for her three books, *English Pleasure Gardens* (1902), *Spanish and Portuguese Gardens* (1924), and *Italian Pleasure Gardens* (1928). In a period of active debate about the direction garden design should be taking—between the romantic and the formal camps—Rose stood firmly on the ground that her mentor Charles Platt had laid out for her. While English gardens were overrated, Rose Nichols argued, those of Spain and Portugal, "though equally beautiful, remain practically unknown." Her second book, *Spanish and Portuguese Gardens*, did much to alter that state of affairs.

Everywhere she traveled Rose was working down her list of gardens to be included in her latest study, and if they were not open to the public she was determined to find her way into them nevertheless. While at work on *Spanish and Portuguese Gardens* she wished to see the palace and gardens of the Quinta Benfica, near Lisbon, and had written to the Marquesa de Fronteira for her permission to visit them. When the Marquesa neglected to favor her with a reply, Rose dressed up in her finest outfit, and asked to be delivered to the gatehouse, where the servants did not dare to turn her away. When the Marquesa appeared in the garden to question this elegant stranger strolling under a parasol through the clipped boxwood, she was instantly impressed with Rose's elegance and authority, and the two women became devoted friends ever after.

No wonder Rose knew so many people everywhere. The artist Polly Thayer, who toured with her through Europe, recalled how the two Boston ladies—one old, the other young—traveled with a frugal purse, eating modestly and finding simple accommodation. "Wherever we went, whomever we met," remembered Thayer, "it was only minutes before Rose was discussing their condition, their politics, and their circumstances." She was at home in any language; though her pronunciation was all her own, her boldness of spirit carried her through.

Rose was also famous for pressing introductions between others she was determined should meet. She was a close friend of her fellow Bostonian, the art historian Bernard Berenson, and rarely failed to call on him in his villa near Florence. But one day when she rang his bell without forewarning him, he sent a message down with the servant that he was "indisposed." Rose, however, was not in a position to be turned away, and knowing that she

Boston hats: the sewing circle at 55 Mount Vernon Street (Rose Nichols is far left), circa 1950s

already had the upper hand, she immediately jotted a note to Berenson, revealing "I have three queens," and sent it up. Berenson looked out the window and saw that Rose was not just playing poker, for there stood Queen Sofia of Greece, Queen Alexandra of Yugoslavia, and Queen Margherita of Italy. Needless to say, all four ladies were escorted in at once.

Home Again

It was Rose Nichols' ultimate goal to preserve the house on Mount Vernon Street as a museum. She would never forget the instructive story of Bernard Berenson, who grew up in Boston's rough West End and took a job delivering newspapers on Beacon Hill. He longed to get into one of the houses, to see what it looked like inside. But there was no open house on Beacon Hill. Future generations might never know how people lived and furnished their houses on Beacon Hill in the early twentieth century. Rose felt strongly that the public should be invited to "see the inside as well as the outside of one of these fine homes."

In the midst of her travels, Rose had for years carried in her mind's eye the vision of her rooms back home in Boston and Cornish, and she was always on the lookout for an interesting bit of furniture here, a sample of fabric there, with which to decorate. "I have bought one large square of printed cotton to try in the Cornish music room," she wrote to her sister Marian. And for 55 Mount

Vernon Street, which the two spinster sisters shared after their parents died (Margaret was married with six children), "some Liberty velveteen for the new room—maroon red, not terra cotta or crimson, a sort of pomegranate." Away for several months at a time, she was diligent in instructing Marian as to the care of the house in Boston and the garden in Cornish: "a dozen or so phlox and larkspur for the garden . . . and I want half a dozen hardy early grapevines started . . . then plant all the usual kinds of seeds not forgetting foxgloves, Canterbury bells and the other biennials. IF YOU PLEASE."

On the rare occasion when Marian was abroad and Rose was home, the instructions continued nevertheless. "Be on the lookout for black oak furniture, hand-made peasant laces and good homespun linen. I should think Denmark would be just the place for any and all of these." Rose firmly believed that you could mix elements from different cultures and periods, as long as they all had quality. It was the same with people. "The finest of everything goes together," she declared with her customary certainty.

In her old age Rose would begin her day in bed under the canopy of her own fine crewel work, with *The New York Times*, *The Wall Street Journal*, and the radio. The telephone was at hand, but when it rang Rose could hardly find it under the mass of books and papers she was in the midst of reading and the piece of embroidery on which she was working. When the mail came at ten o'clock Mary King would deliver it to Rose's bedside along with her morning eggnog, spiked with a jigger of sherry.

By the end of her traveling days, Rose had mellowed. Having lived through two world wars, world peace was her primary concern. Her idea was to connect to the enemy or adversary by confronting him, arguing if you had to, and ultimately to find common ground through a mutual love of gardens, art, architecture, and in the sharing of a pot of tea. There is no precise recipe for Rose Nichols' gathering of minds, for every tea party contained different ingredients and unpredictable combinations. Add a dash of the sweet to the savory, mix the frivolous with the frugal, the glamorous with the plain, the old with the young, and something interesting—in the best Boston tradition—is bound to happen.

Part Two

Recipes & Reminiscences

Not long ago, recipes were written in the simplest form. Most were so basic as to list ingredients by "pinches" and "handfuls." Baking instructions were often as plain as "bake quick" or "cook until done." Perhaps cooks of the past needed fewer instructions than our chefs of today. Certainly stove temperatures varied to a greater degree. In any case, to be in step with modern practice, we have tested the old-style recipes and made them longer with more detail, in the hope that not too much will be left to guesswork. We do so with regret, for we miss the quaintness and simplicity of the originals. They are another relic of a time gone by.

For these six teas, we have included many recipes from the file of Mary King, Rose Nichols' cook, and some from the Platt House in Cornish. We have rounded out the collection with a few period recipes and some from the authors' families.

A Beacon Hill Tea

"There are few hours
in life more agreeable
than the hour dedicated
to the ceremony known
as Afternoon Tea."

—Henry James,
Portrait of a Lady, 1881

A
Beacon Hill Tea
Menu

Apricot Meringue Squares

Fairy Gingerbread

Glazed Orange Cake

Broccoli Sandwiches

Mushroom Roll-ups or Sandwiches

Curried Chicken Sandwiches

Pilgrim's Punch

Hu-Kwa Tea
The robust smoky tea comparable to a rich old Bordeaux

"*Four o'clock sharp,*" *Mary King, cook and housekeeper at 55 Mount Vernon Street, recounted. "Sometimes twelve, fifteen, eighteen men and women. Young and old. She'd get somebody started, you know, on politics or international things, and then it all went along. Sometimes they'd be here until eight in the evening. She'd have Harvard professors and neighbors, and if somebody new came and she didn't like them, they wouldn't get asked again. Just once they came."*

Rose Nichols, although certainly a skilled hostess, did not trouble herself with less cerebral culinary matters. "She couldn't burn water," Mary recalled with affection, in an interview given many years later, after Rose Nichols' death. And so it was Mary, each Sunday, who saw that the tea table was properly laid out with appropriate teatime fare and steeped strong Hu-Kwa tea that rivaled in potency the intellectual brew stirred up by Miss Rose's cunningly "mismatched" assemblages.

Apricot Meringue Squares

Mary King used apricot jam in the original recipe, but we found that we did not have as sweet a tooth as Miss Rose and replaced the jam with dried apricots. You may wish to experiment with other dried fruit. These delicious squares should be served cut into dainty 1½- to 2-inch pieces.

  1½ cups diced dried apricots
    1 cup orange juice
    1 tablespoon lemon juice
      Water
    1 cup flour, sifted
  ½ teaspoon salt
  ¼ teaspoon baking soda
    1 stick softened, unsalted butter
  ½ cup sugar
    1 teaspoon grated lemon zest
    3 large eggs, separated
  ¼ cup sugar (for meringue)
  ½ cup finely chopped, unsalted nuts

Preheat oven to 350° F. • Place fruit, orange juice, and lemon juice into a small saucepan, and add enough water to cover the fruit. Partially cover the pan, and simmer until liquid is completely absorbed and fruit is soft. If necessary, add more water. Set aside to cool. • In a separate bowl, sift together flour, salt, and baking soda. Set aside. • In a large bowl, cream the butter, sugar, and lemon zest thoroughly. Add egg yolks one at a time, beating well after each addition. Add flour mixture and work in until just combined.

The Boston Hat

The Boston headgear favored by ladies of Rose Nichols' generation was justifiably famous, and Rose Nichols' hats were no exception. It was Beacon Hill denizen Frances Howard who wrote of one Boston lady who, when asked by an awed observer where she bought hers, replied: "Where do I buy my hats? Oh, we don't *buy* our hats—we *have* our hats."

"A look at a good dressy winter hat on a Boston woman induces the thought that they are indeed worth preserving —built for long wear, like the mohair sofa and the horsehair armchairs in the livingroom— not to be lightly discarded like the flimsier transient whimsies of New York."

Frances Howard, *Beacon Hill, The Hub of the Universe*

25

The dough will be soft. For ease of handling, refrigerate for 20 to 30 minutes. • Grease two 8" square pans and press half the dough into each pan. (We suggest placing a piece of plastic wrap over the surface of the dough to keep it from sticking to your hands, and to make the task of spreading it evenly much easier.) Remove plastic and spread the fruit mixture over the dough, making certain that it reaches the edges.

For the meringue, using an electric mixer, beat egg whites until soft peaks form. Gradually add the remaining ¼ cup of sugar and beat until stiff peaks form. Fold in nuts. Spread meringue over fruit. The meringue should completely cover the fruit. • Bake for 25 minutes, or until the meringue starts to color. Cool and cut into bite-size squares.

The squares can be made 24 hours in advance of serving, covered loosely with aluminum foil and stored in a cool (not refrigerated) location. They will also keep for one week in an airtight container, packed between layers of waxed paper, although you may find that the meringue has softened somewhat.

Yield: Approximately 70

Fairy Gingerbread

It would seem most likely that the "Fairy" in this recipe's title refers to the lightness, such a gossamer texture that it occasioned

"We must always remember that it is a great merit in housekeeping to manage a little well. Economy and frugality must never, however, be allowed to degenerate into parsimony and meanness."

Mrs. Beeton, *Beeton's Book of Household Management*

one tea party guest to acclaim: "It's so light—it almost floats." Although Mary called this recipe "gingerbread," we are more apt to regard these tea treats as cookies.

1¼ cups sifted flour
1½ teaspoons ground ginger
1 stick softened, unsalted butter
¾ cup granulated brown sugar
½ cup milk

Preheat oven to 450° F. • Combine flour and ginger and sift into a medium bowl. Set aside. • In a large bowl, using an electric beater, cream butter and sugar until fluffy. Add the flour mixture in three batches and beat to combine. The dough will form clumps. Gradually add milk and beat until the batter is smooth. • Thoroughly grease an 11" x 17" rimmed cookie pan and pour batter into pan, spreading evenly to edges. • Bake for 7 minutes and remove from oven. The gingerbread will be lightly colored around the edges. • Score into small squares by marking with a sharp knife. Return to oven and bake for a few more minutes or until the center portion of the dough is lightly colored. Cut neatly along the scored lines. Using a metal spatula, carefully remove cookies from the pan to racks. Cool thoroughly. • The cookies will keep for at least one week in an airtight container or sealed plastic bags. They may be frozen for one month.

Yield: Approximately 50 to 60

The Boston Purse

From time to time the Boston purse will open for certain worthy causes and cultural benevolences. It does not, however, hang agape.

December 19, 1893

Dear Rose,

. . . It is absolutely important to make the best use of your advantages and if that includes one or two new dresses which you can buy at reasonable cost, it is best to get them. But it is important not to spend in such a way as to make the rest of your party in any degree uncomfortable. Of course a great variety in the way of dresses is not expected of travelers, and if you do not stay very long in one place, no one can get very tired of your clothes except yourselves, and that does not matter much. . . .
—E. F. N.

Elizabeth Nichols, to her daughter Rose in Europe

Glazed Orange Cake

2 sticks softened, unsalted butter
2 cups sugar
1 teaspoon vanilla
2 tablespoons finely grated orange zest
5 large eggs
3 cups cake flour, sifted
½ teaspoon salt
1 tablespoon baking powder
¾ cup milk
   Glaze:
4 tablespoons unsalted butter
⅔ cup white granulated sugar
⅓ cup orange juice concentrate

Preheat oven to 350° F. • In a large mixing bowl, use electric mixer to cream butter and sugar until light and fluffy. Add vanilla and orange zest and combine thoroughly. Add eggs, one at a time, beating each in well. • Combine flour, baking powder, and salt and sift into wet ingredients, adding the milk gradually as you mix. • Grease a 10" tubular pan and dust with flour. Pour in batter and bake for 1 hour or until a wooden skewer inserted into the center of the cake comes out clean. Leave cake in pan until cooled. Unmold onto plate.

Glaze: Heat ingredients for glaze until sugar is dissolved and slowly pour glaze over top. If the cake is not served right away, wrap carefully in aluminum foil. It will keep for one week stored in a cool place.

Yield: Approximately 35 thin slices

Broccoli Sandwiches

Even today this is a sought-after and guarded recipe on Beacon Hill. The use of broccoli places these sandwiches into the "secret recipe" category. No one can guess the source of the tang.

    2 medium heads broccoli
    2 sticks softened, unsalted butter
    1½ cups mayonnaise (homemade would be preferable—
        but a generous squeeze of lemon juice will brighten up
        most store-bought brands)
    2 loaves thin-sliced white bread, crusts removed

Purchase fresh broccoli that has firm green florets. Using a sharp knife, shave florets off broccoli heads onto a plate. • Thinly coat bread slices on one side only with softened butter. • Generously spread buttered side of bread slices with mayonnaise. Be more generous with the mayonnaise than you might otherwise be, as the mayonnaise needs to "pick up" the broccoli. • Place bread slice, mayonnaise side down, into broccoli. Gently tap bread and remove. You should have a thin even coat of florets. Place a second slice of bread (also spread with mayonnaise) on top. Slice into rectangles. Store and chill as directed on page 106.

A Frugal Thought: Leftover broccoli stalks may be chopped and added to soup, or if pared to reveal the core, they are very tender and may be eaten raw or used with dip.

Yield: Approximately 60

The Boston Dress

Brahmin women, never considered paragons of fashion, shopped at R.H. Stearns for dresses and Wethern's for hats. They preferred pearl chokers, low-heeled shoes, and long-sleeved nightgowns.

The Nature of Massachusetts

December 19, 1893

Dear Rose,

*. . . You will be amused to hear about my dress. Last week, when [the seamstress] was here, I took out my old plum-colored silk dress, which I brought from Paris fifteen years ago, and concluded it could be made presentable. So I bought velvet enough for new sleeves and a little cape or ruffle . . . then at Aunt Genie's suggestion we took out the white lace in the neck and sleeves and put in black lace, and it is really a very stylish and becoming dress much admired by family and friends.
—E. F. N.*

Elizabeth Nichols, to her daughter Rose in Europe

29

Mushroom Roll-ups or Sandwiches

When Mary King made these sandwiches, she had only the ubiquitous button mushroom. Now, years later, we have a large variety of wild and tastier fungi from which to choose.

1 pound fresh mushrooms, finely chopped (for more flavor, we recommend combining regular button mushrooms with a portion of Japanese shitake mushrooms)
1 stick softened, unsalted butter (plus extra butter for coating bread)
1 cup light cream
3 teaspoons sifted flour
¾ teaspoon salt
2 teaspoons finely chopped chives
1 teaspoon lemon juice
1½ loaves thin-sliced white bread, crusts removed

In a large skillet, melt butter. Sauté mushrooms in butter over low heat for approximately 8 minutes, stirring occasionally. They will render their juices, and then reabsorb them. Set aside. • In a separate bowl, thoroughly blend sifted flour into light cream and add to the mushroom mixture in the skillet. Cook over low heat and stir until thickened. • Add salt, chives, and lemon juice to skillet. Stir to combine. Set aside to cool to room temperature. • Butter one side of bread slice and spread enough mushroom mixture to evenly coat each slice of bread and roll up in jellyroll fashion. • Slice each roll into thirds. However, if you plan to freeze them (they will keep well in the freezer for one month), leave whole. Defrost and slice just before serving.

This delicious mushroom filling may also be used as a tea sandwich filling. If you make sandwiches, cut into three rectangles and serve as soon as possible. You may also freeze the filling separately for up to three months and defrost and reheat slowly in a saucepan when needed for sandwiches or roll-ups.

A Frugal Thought: If you have mushroom filling left over, it may be frozen and used to enrich and thicken soups and sauces. It is also delicious as a topping for toast.

Yield: Approximately 70

Curried Chicken Sandwiches

Author's family recipe

4 cups cooked chopped chicken, white meat is preferable
½ cup good Indian chutney, finely chopped
½ cup chopped almonds or peanuts
1 tablespoon finely chopped chives
1 to 1½ cups good mayonnaise (homemade would be preferable
    —but a generous squeeze of lemon juice will brighten up
    most store-bought brands)
2 tablespoons good-quality curry powder
2 tablespoons peanut oil
1 stick softened, unsalted butter
1½ loaves whole oat bread, crusts removed (not thinly sliced
    bread)

In a large bowl, combine chopped chicken meat with Indian chutney, almonds and chives. Set aside. • To curry the mayonnaise: warm peanut oil in a skillet over low heat and add curry powder, stirring to release the curry flavor for approximately a minute. Set aside to cool. Blend into the mayonnaise. • Make sandwiches by buttering the inner sides of two slices of bread and coating with curried chicken mixture. • Cut into thirds. Refrigerate until ½ hour before serving. For convenience, you can make the curried chicken spread one or two days in advance.

Yield: Approximately 42

Pilgrim's Punch

You may find that the punch recipes, or "frappés," as Rose's mother, Elizabeth Nichols, called them at her 1893 Christmas tea, are too sweet for today's tastes. If so, adjust the recipes by reducing some of the sweeter ingredients. We have included punch recipes in our tea menus for the benefit of members of the younger generation, who may not yet have acquired a taste for tea.

    1 cup water
    2 cups sugar
    1 quart strawberries
    1 cup strong tea (not Hu-Kwa)
      Juice of 4 oranges
      Juice of 2 lemons

2 cups pineapple juice (unsweetened if you like)
1 quart lemon sorbet
1 quart cold water
1 quart carbonated water

In a medium saucepan, stir the water with the sugar over moderate heat until sugar has completely dissolved, then boil for approximately 5 minutes to make a sugar syrup. • Press fresh or unsweetened frozen strawberries through a sieve to extract the juice. • Combine sugar syrup, strawberry juice, tea, orange juice, lemon juice, and pineapple juice. Let stand. You may refrigerate the liquid for 24 hours in a tightly covered, non-metallic container. • When you are ready to serve, strain liquid over lemon sorbet that has been placed into a large, chilled punch bowl. Add cold water and carbonated water. Garnish with a few small perfect strawberries and a few mint leaves.

Yield: Approximately 20 cups

A Cornish Tea

"The cup of tea on arrival at a
country house is a thing which,
as a rule, I particularly enjoy—
the crackling logs—shaded light—
the scent of buttered toast—
the general atmosphere of
leisured cosiness."

—P.G. Wodehouse,
The Code of the Woosters, 1938

A
Cornish Tea
Menu

Delicate Cake

Aunt Alice Cole's Almond Cake

Nun's Puffs

Butter Drops

New Hampshire Seed Cookies

Radish & Watercress Sandwiches

Emerald Ice

China Oolong Tea
*A large-leaf tea with a hint of green in its amber color—
a unique tea whose flavor resembles no other*

Encuraged by her favorite Uncle Augustus and Aunt Augusta Saint-Gaudens, in 1892 Rose Nichols and her family became summer residents of Cornish, New Hampshire. By this time, Cornish had been established as a full-fledged artists' colony, alive with Bohemian, free-spirited energy that perhaps would have scandalized the sedate Bostonians with whom the Nichols family socialized during the remainder of the year.

Once settled in Cornish at "Mastlands," the family joined a lively and active circle. Depending on the season's available light, both artists and gardeners alike broke from work almost daily at 4:00 in the afternoon to gather on piazzas or in gardens for tea and conversation. Often games, gossip, and the airing of ongoing feuds between artists would keep the colony humming well into the night. Invitations for lunches and formal dinners were issued and answered, and Rose soon learned that possessing a biting wit and keen intelligence would secure her a place at most tables.

The transplanted members of Boston's Teacup Society would often quench their thirsts at The Tea Tray, the popular tea house distinctly identified by its double-sided sign painted by colonist Maxfield Parrish. As he had done in so many of his works, Parrish portrayed his favorite local model (and later mistress), Sue Lewin, as both the male and female figures on the sign. From 1913 to 1915, this local landmark was further distinguished when it became a favorite stop for President and Mrs. Woodrow Wilson when the Summer White House moved to Cornish.

March 1894

Dear Rose,

Yesterday I began work on the large spruce spar that encumbered the field south of the main piazza. This flag-staff, when completed, will form a prominent landmark at the triangle where our land begins. When you see this lofty mast in the distance, you will know where you are.
—A. H. N.

Dr. Nichols, to his daughter Rose

Delicate Cake

This Cornish recipe produces two excellent, fine-textured cakes. You will find that the recipe is easier to make using a standing mixer. If you prefer a hand-held beater, we suggest halving the ingredients to make one loaf at a time.

    8 large egg whites
    1 cup light cream
    1 teaspoon rose water (or extract flavoring of your choice)
    2 cups superfine sugar
 3½ cups cake flour, sifted
    ½ teaspoon baking soda
    2 sticks unsalted butter cut into tablespoon-size pieces,
       at room temperature

Preheat oven to 350° F. • In a large bowl, lightly whisk egg whites, cream, and flavoring. Set aside. • In the bowl of a standing mixer, beat together the sugar, flour, and baking soda. • Gradually add the butter pieces to the dry ingredients. Mix at a medium-low speed to incorporate. • Add half the cream and egg-white mixture and beat at medium speed for 1 to 2 minutes. Scrape the sides of the bowl and gradually add the remaining mixture, beating it in well. • Bake the cake in two 6-cup loaf pans (approximately 9½" x 5½" x 3"). You may also use two fluted tube pans with a 6-cup capacity. *Note:* If using loaf pans, grease pans first, then line with waxed paper. Grease the waxed paper and dust with flour. If using tube pans, grease and dust with flour. • When a wooden skewer inserted in the center comes out clean, the cakes are done. Let rest for 10 minutes, and remove cakes from pans, using a thin-bladed knife to dislodge them, if necessary. Let cool to room temperature.

"Few parts of New England bear so strong a resemblance to an Italian landscape as the hills rising above the banks of Mount Ascutney. . . . Those who were so fortunate as to dwell there thirty or forty years ago will never forget the joys of those early days and the friendly intercourse between the enterprising pioneers. Apart from the practice of his own particular art each was intent upon making his place a little paradise. . . . Every householder was his own head gardener and landscape architect, though subject to much constructive criticism from his neighbors."

Rose Nichols, "A Hilltop Garden in New Hampshire," *The House Beautiful*, 1902

On first sight, Augustus Saint-Gaudens had not been captivated by his newly purchased property in Cornish: "My dwelling looked as if it had been abandoned for it stood out … gaunt, austere and forbidding without a trace of charm. And the longer I stayed in it, the more its Puritanical austerity irritated me."

Despite early misgivings, the property, with its newly created grapevine-hung terraces and skillfully landscaped gardens, was to become his permanent home, Aspet—a place for work and restoration of spirit he could find nowhere else. In 1907, Saint-Gaudens died and was buried there. Since 1965 this residence has been a National Historic Site, and well worth a visit to see firsthand not only what had attracted artists to Cornish, but what held them there.

The cakes may be made up to two days in advance, wrapped in airtight containers and stored at room temperature. These cakes may also be frozen for several months.

Yield: 2 loaves

Aunt Alice Cole's Almond Cake

The ground almonds stirred into the batter of this cake provide an interesting crunchy texture. The unusual gelatin glaze gives the top of the cake a crystalline shimmer and acts as a base to keep the almonds in place. This recipe makes two cakes.

    8 large egg whites
    2 teaspoons almond extract
    3 cups sifted cake flour
    1 teaspoon cream of tartar
    2 cups superfine sugar
    2 sticks unsalted butter at room temperature, cut into
       tablespoon-size pieces
    ½ teaspoon baking soda
    3 tablespoons milk
    ½ cup toasted blanched almonds, finely ground

Glaze:
   6 tablespoons cool water
   2 teaspoons unflavored gelatin
1½ cups superfine sugar
  ¾ cup toasted sliced blanched almonds

Preheat oven to 350° F. • In a medium bowl, using a whisk, combine egg whites and almond extract. Set aside. • In a large bowl of a standing electric mixer, mix together the flour, cream of tartar, and sugar. Add the butter pieces to the dry ingredients and beat at low speed until butter is dispersed. The mixture will not be smooth. • Add half the egg-white mixture and beat at medium speed for 1 minute, scraping down the bowl as necessary. Gradually add the remaining egg whites, and continue to beat at medium-high speed for 2 more minutes, scraping down bowl. (If you are using a hand-held beater, add another minute to the final beating time.) • In a cup, stir baking soda into milk and add to the cake batter mixture. Blend thoroughly. Fold ground almonds into the batter. Make sure they are evenly distributed. • Grease two 9" round cake pans, and line the bottoms with waxed paper. Grease again, then dust with flour. Divide batter equally between the two pans. • Bake cakes 35 to 45 minutes, or until a wooden skewer comes out clean. Remove from oven and let rest for 15 minutes. Loosen cakes from the sides of the pan with a sharp, thin-bladed knife, and turn the cakes out onto a rack. Peel off waxed paper, and invert each cake. Let cool to room temperature. When cakes are completely cool, apply glaze.

The American Renaissance

A prime example of the artistic talent and accomplishments of the Cornish Colony —the movement known as the "American Renaissance" —is shown to its fullest throughout the Boston Public Library, located in Copley Square, a pleasant walk from the Nichols House Museum. See *A Suggested Tour* on page 122.

Glaze (to be applied at least 4 hours before you plan to serve the cake): Place water in a small saucepan. Stir in gelatin, and let soften for 5 minutes. Place pan over low heat and stir until the gelatin is dissolved. Gradually beat sugar into gelatin, using a whisk. The mixture will become thick and begin to stiffen. Remove from heat.
• Using a rubber spatula, apply a thin coat of glaze to each cake and sprinkle with thinly sliced toasted almonds. You should plan to serve the cakes the same day you glaze them.

The unglazed cakes may be stored tightly wrapped, at room temperature, for up to two days. Freeze unglazed cakes in an airtight container. They will keep for up to one month.

Yield: Two 9-inch round cakes

Nun's Puffs

Served warm out of the oven and accompanied by sweet butter and a good homemade preserve, these little puffs make a tasty and charming addition to the breakfast table, as well as for tea.

   1 cup milk
   1 stick unsalted butter, cut into pieces
2½ cups flour, sifted
  ¼ teaspoon salt
   4 large eggs, separated

Preheat oven to 400° F. • In a small saucepan scald milk by gently heating until a skin forms on the top. Add butter pieces to the hot milk and stir until melted. Set aside. • Place sifted flour in a medium bowl and add salt. • Using an electric beater, gradually beat milk into the flour mixture, beating until smooth. Add egg yolks and beat well. • In a medium bowl, whisk or beat egg whites to the soft-peak stage. Add a quarter of the egg whites to batter and stir to thoroughly combine. Fold in remaining egg whites until thoroughly combined. • Carefully spoon the batter into well-greased mini-muffin pans; fill to three-quarters full. Bake at 400° F for 10 minutes, reduce heat to 350° F, and continue baking for an additional 20 minutes or until puffs are just beginning to turn a golden color. Remove from pan and serve while still warm.

Note: The batter may be made up to two hours in advance and kept covered in a cool place or refrigerated. Although definitely not as good as served right from the oven, Nun's Puffs may be baked and held at room temperature for several hours and then reheated in a 300° F oven for five minutes to crisp.

Yield: Approximately 50

Butter Drops

This is such a good basic cookie recipe, it should be in everyone's repertoire. To liven up the flavor, add half a teaspoon of pure lime

New Hampshire's Lincoln

In conversation with his good friend Charles C. Beaman, New York financier and Cornish summer resident, Saint-Gaudens had bemoaned his inability to find a model for a statue of Lincoln. Beaman is said to have enticed Saint-Gaudens to Cornish with the promise that craggy, Lincoln-esque men could be easily found in the surrounding foot-hills of Mount Ascutney. This promise was fulfilled in the form of Langdon Morse, whose remarkable likeness to Lincoln was captured in Saint-Gaudens' model for the Stand-ing Lincoln statue in Chicago's Lincoln Park.

Cornish Dress

At dinner, tea, or a picnic, women were expected to wear something pretty, artistic, or both—no widow's black was sanctioned. It was Cornish resident and prolific sculptor Herbert Adams who admonished the women of the Colony to "be careful what they wore to picnics...that they should wear white or bright colors."

Herbert Adams' bronze of the Unitarian reformer, William Ellery Channing, minister, abolitionist, and author of the book *Slavery*, is located at the corner of Boston's Public Garden, facing his Arlington Street Church. See *A Suggested Tour* on page 122.

or lemon extract, and then coat with tangy lemon frosting. These cookies are easy to prepare.

1 stick unsalted butter
1½ cups powdered sugar
Juice of 3 limes and their zest, grated (about 2 tablespoons)
(or ½ teaspoon of lemon or lime extract)
1 large egg
¼ teaspoon salt
2½ cups sifted flour
1 teaspoon baking soda
1 teaspoon cream of tartar

Lemon Frosting:
½ cup powdered sugar
1 tablespoon fresh lemon juice, or enough to make the frosting spreadable

Preheat oven to 350° F. • In a large mixing bowl, using an electric beater, cream butter, adding sugar gradually until light and fluffy. Add juice and zest of limes and when thoroughly blended, mix in unbeaten egg. • Sift the remaining dry ingredients together and blend well into creamed mixture. • Grease a cookie sheet. If the dough is too soft, chill until firm enough to form into ½" balls. Leave space as the cookies will spread to 1½" in diameter. Bake 10 minutes or until lightly colored. Completely cool on wire racks before frosting.

Lemon Frosting: You should frost the cookies the same day you plan to serve them. To make lemon frosting, mix powdered sugar with lemon juice and enough water to make a thin frosting. Using a brush, coat tops of cookies lightly with frosting and allow it to set. The cookies may be kept for one week in an airtight container. Unfrosted, they may be frozen for approximately one month. Thaw uncovered at room temperature.

Yield: Approximately 80

New Hampshire Seed Cookies

Sesame originated in Africa and was first planted in the United States by Thomas Jefferson at Monticello. The use of sesame seeds in New England kitchens became well established by the mid-nineteenth century.

¾ cup toasted hulled sesame seeds (The use of hulled sesame seeds is key, as seeds with hulls will produce a strong taste. Hulled sesame seeds can usually be found in Asian markets.)
1½ sticks softened, unsalted butter
1½ cups tightly packed brown sugar
  2 large eggs
1¼ cups flour
  ¼ teaspoon baking powder
  1 teaspoon vanilla

Preheat oven to 325° F. • Toast hulled seeds in a large, heavy skillet over low heat, by shaking and stirring the pan every few seconds until seeds turn light brown and begin to glisten, about 5 to 7 minutes. Remove pan from heat and continue stirring for a minute to cool seeds. Remove seeds to a small bowl. Set aside. • In a large mixing bowl, using an electric beater, cream together butter and brown sugar. Add eggs and beat well. Set aside. • Sift together flour and baking powder over creamed mixture; blend well. Add ½ cup toasted sesame seeds and vanilla; blend thoroughly. If the dough is too soft, chill until firm enough to form ½″ balls. Dip each ball—one side only—into a dish containing remaining sesame seeds. • Place seeded side up, approximately 1½″ apart on ungreased cookie sheet, leaving space for cookies to spread. Bake for 10 to 15 minutes or until cookie edges are light brown and firm to the touch. • Cool thoroughly on wire racks before storing in airtight containers for approximately one week. They may be frozen for up to one month.

Yield: Approximately 80

Radish & Watercress Sandwiches

⅓ cup watercress leaves, finely chopped
3 tablespoons softened, unsalted butter
5 or 6 large radishes, finely chopped
1 loaf thin-sliced white bread, crusts removed

In a food processor combine watercress and softened butter and chop to a fine consistency. • Mince radishes in a food processor or chop by hand. • To make sandwiches, spread watercress and butter mixture on a slice of bread and sprinkle minced radishes to evenly coat. Top with a slice of bread and cut into three rectangles.

Yield: Approximately 48

Emerald Ice

½ cup very good mint jelly (not too sweet)
½ cup water
2 tablespoons strongly brewed tea (not Hu-Kwa)
3 tablespoons fresh lime juice
1 quart good lemon sorbet or ice (homemade is best)
1 quart carbonated water, chilled
  Sugar to taste
  Lime slices for garnish
  Chilled punch bowl

Combine mint jelly and water in a small saucepan and cook over medium heat for 5 minutes to make a syrup. Add brewed tea and stir. Chill. (This syrup will keep for one week, tightly covered in the refrigerator.) • When ready to serve, mound lemon ice into chilled punch bowl and add cooled mint jelly syrup mixture, fresh lime juice, and carbonated water. Taste, and add sugar if needed. Stir and serve immediately. Garnish with thin slices of lime.

Yield: 16 cups

A European Tea

"We both need to come in contact with warm responsive natives to counteract the effect of too much Boston."

—Rose Nichols writing to her sister Marian from Rome, 1896

A
European Tea
Menu

Lemon Verbena Little Cakes

Sponge Drops

Swedish Wafers

English Pound Cake

Nut & Fruit Sandwiches

Olive, Anchovy, & Watercress Sandwiches

Egg, Pimento, & Caper Sandwiches

Earl Grey Tea

A black tea with the flowery scent of Bergamot,
"Citrus Bergamia," the oil or dried flower which imparts the special flavor

Society and touring may have taken Rose Nichols to Europe, but her writing on landscape design kept her returning for many years. All three of her garden books, sadly now out of print, presented gardens as seen through her unique lens not only as landscape designer, but also as architect, historian, artist, and photographer. Her first book, English Pleasure Gardens, *written in 1902, included nearly 300 of her drawings, site plans, and photographs. Her last book,* Italian Pleasure Gardens, *published in 1928, covered the height and breadth of Italy, from Pompeii to the Middle Ages on through the Renaissance to the Baroque. But, undoubtedly, Rose Nichols' gift to our knowledge of gardens and their history was her second book,* Spanish and Portuguese Gardens, *published in 1924.*

From Portugal she wrote of the colorful impressions of local surroundings. "In the afternoon, although the Mid-Lent Carnival crowded the streets with revelers dressed in fantastic costume, I started out on a garden hunt to my first objective. . . . Upon entering the large garden, through a door in the wall . . . the beauty and the novelty of the scene almost took my breath away. It had a character all its own, and recalled nothing that I had seen in my travels. . . . Every idea had been freely translated into a style that was essentially Portuguese. The whole effect was delightfully spontaneous, showing a knowledge of the past, but no subservience to tradition."

Rose Nichols' travels abroad, however, were never all work. Society piqued her interest just as much as gaining access to an undocumented garden. So it should be mentioned that accounts of dances, dinners, and teas punctuated letters Rose wrote home to her mother and sisters from

"Now while you are Abroad, do let yourself go. Just feel the beauty and take it straight."

Rose, to her sister Marian,
July 1, 1898

Austria, Italy, or Spain, as well as from more exotic locales in Egypt or Morocco. There were many occasions during her travels when social duty called, and Rose repaid an invitation to lunch or dinner by giving little, or even large teas, which befitted both her habit and her small New England purse.

Lemon Verbena Little Cakes

Hotel Palumbo
Ravello, Italy
May 7, 1908

Dear Miss Nichols,

I have to thank you for word of this delightful place. We have been here for a week now and I think we shall be here for several more. The Palumbo is so small and so clean and the cook is really not to be despised. I think you are mighty unselfish to tell anyone about Ravello. I should not blame you if you had tried to keep it as much a secret as possible. . . . Miss McClure begs me to remember her to you most cordially. She shares with me your benefactions.

Faithfully,
Willa Sibert Cather

Literary editor, *McClure's Magazine*, as well as Rose Nichols' editor and friend.

While Rose was traveling in Italy these tiny verbena cakes may have appeared at tea time. Lemon verbena can be found abroad throughout the warmer climes and its taste evokes the Mediterranean's herb-scented air.

About lemon verbena: Contents of two lemon verbena teabags (soaked in water until soft) have been successfully used as a substitute. Fresh lemon verbena, however, is available in temperate climates, and may be purchased at wholesale produce markets at various times of the year. Lemon thyme and lavender flower buds also make excellent substitutes, obtainable at many health food stores. *You should only use fresh herbs that have not been sprayed with chemicals. Health food stores are a good resource for this type of provision.*

    1 cup cake flour
    ½ teaspoon baking powder
    ¼ teaspoon salt
    3 tablespoons finely chopped fresh or dried lemon verbena
    1 tablespoon freshly grated lemon zest
    1½ sticks unsalted butter, softened
    1 cup sugar
    3 large eggs
    ¾ teaspoon vanilla
    2 tablespoons milk
    2 tablespoons fresh lemon juice

      Glaze:
    ½ cup powdered sugar
    2 tablespoons freshly squeezed lemon juice

Preheat oven to 325° F. • Combine flour, baking powder, and salt, and sift into a large bowl. Add verbena and grated lemon zest. Set aside. • Using an electric beater, cream butter with sugar in a large mixing bowl until light and fluffy. Add eggs one at a time, beating in well after each addition. Blend in vanilla. • Beat in half of the dry ingredients, adding milk and lemon juice gradually. Add the remainder of the dry ingredients, beating until batter is well blended. • Grease a non-stick mini-muffin pan and dust with flour. • Spoon batter carefully into the mini-cups, fill three-quarters full, and smooth tops with a knife. Bake on the middle rack of the oven for 25 to 30 minutes, or until lightly browned and a wooden skewer inserted into the center of a mini-cake comes out clean.

Glaze: In a small bowl, whisk powdered sugar and lemon juice until a thin liquid glaze is formed. While cakes are in the pan and are still hot, drizzle glaze over tops. Cool and remove from pans and serve. If the cakes will not be served immediately, they may be kept stored in the pan or removed and carefully placed between layers of waxed paper in an airtight tin. They will keep at room temperature for five days. They may be frozen for one month and thawed at room temperature.

Yield: Approximately 40

Sponge Drops

These little drops resemble light and airy meringues, but possess their very own mystique. It is best to bake them on a dry day, as you would meringue. Humidity will retard their becoming crisp.

   1 cup sugar (plus extra sugar for sprinkling)
   ½ cup flour
      Pinch of salt
   5 large eggs, separated
      Juice and grated zest of 1 lemon
   ¼ cup finely ground unsalted almonds

Preheat oven to 350° F. • In a small bowl, sift together sugar, flour, and salt. Set aside. • In a large bowl, use an electric mixer to beat egg yolks at low speed for about 30 seconds. Gradually add dry ingredients, and beat at medium speed, scraping down bowl as needed. • In a separate bowl, beat egg whites until they form soft peaks. • Add a quarter of the egg whites to egg-yolk mixture, and fold in. Continue to fold in remaining egg whites. • Line a large cookie sheet with parchment paper. Using non-stick cooking spray, heavily coat parchment. Drop scant teaspoonfuls of batter on baking sheet, and sprinkle each lightly with sugar. Bake for 8 to 10 minutes, watching carefully as the drops burn easily. When they are barely beginning to color around the edges, remove from oven. • Using a sharp, thin-bladed spatula, place cookies on wire racks to cool completely. Store up to two days in an airtight container at room temperature, with waxed paper placed between the layers. Freeze, wrapped airtight, for up to one month.

Yield: Approximately 120

Swedish Wafers

It was a surprise, even to us, to find that these delicate cookies may be stored for up to one month if placed between layers of waxed paper in an airtight cookie tin and kept in a dry cool area. We also like to give these cookies as gifts at Christmas—when dusted with powdered sugar they look like pretty snowflakes.

¾ cup finely ground unsalted almonds
½ cup sugar
1 tablespoon flour
2 tablespoons milk
1 stick unsalted butter
Powdered sugar

Preheat oven to 350° F. • In a medium bowl, mix almonds, sugar, flour, and milk until thoroughly combined. • Place butter in a small heavy saucepan and add the almond-flour mixture. Cook over low heat until the butter has melted. • Grease large cookie sheet and dust with flour. Drop mixture by teaspoon onto cookie sheet. Bake for 7 minutes. Watch carefully—the cookies should be only slightly browned at edges. • Remove cookie sheet from oven and cool for a minute or two. Using a sharp thin-bladed spatula, quickly test to see if cookies can be removed easily, and if so, working rapidly, remove each cookie carefully to cool on a wire rack. If cookies are difficult to remove, you may need to cool them longer or, alternatively, put them back into the oven for a few minutes. As you become more familiar with this recipe, you will determine which method works better for you. Powdered sugar may be sifted over cookies before storing.

Yield: Approximately 75

"Before going to Portugal, the little republic west of Spain seemed very remote and was chiefly associated in my mind with earthquakes and revolution. It seemed to be still, as Lord Byron called it . . . a 'purple land where law secures not life.' But during my visit, no evidence of political excitement was apparent, while its romantic history, characteristic architecture, and exquisitely beautiful scenery were a revelation. The Moorish occupation . . . and intercourse with India, Brazil, and Morocco . . . have left their traces, without exercising a too obvious influence. Fortunately, little countries, like small people, often make up in charm and individuality for what they lack in size."

Rose Nichols, *Spanish and Portuguese Gardens*, 1924

53

English Pound Cake

The pound cake, English or otherwise, seems to have its ups and downs in the world of food fashion. At the moment it is making a comeback. Its reappearance on menus in the finer establishments was inevitable, for a well-made pound cake, in its modest way, has a lot to offer. When properly made, it allows accompanying flavors to shine.

To create a pound cake of the desired texture, the butter, eggs, and milk **must** *all be at room temperature before you begin.*

    3 large eggs
    6 tablespoons milk
    ¾ teaspoon vanilla
    1½ cups cake flour
    ½ teaspoon salt
    1½ teaspoons baking powder
    1 cup superfine sugar
    1½ sticks softened, unsalted butter
    ½ teaspoon finely grated lemon zest

Preheat oven to 325° F. • In a small bowl, combine eggs, milk, and vanilla. Whisk lightly and set aside. • In a large bowl, combine flour, salt, baking powder, and sugar; sift twice. Add butter cut into tablespoon-size pieces. Using an electric beater, beat at low speed for about 30 seconds, just to disperse butter. The mixture will not be smooth. • Add half the whisked egg-milk mixture and beat at medium speed until batter is smooth. Now beat at high speed for one minute, scraping down bowl, as needed. Continue to beat at a high speed, gradually adding remaining egg mixture, beating until well blended. Carefully fold in lemon zest. • Grease and line an 8" x 4" loaf pan with waxed paper, and grease again. Dust with flour and pour batter into pan. • Bake 45 to 50 minutes, or until a wooden skewer inserted in the center comes out clean. Let cool in pan for 10 minutes. Remove cake from pan and peel off paper. Cool on wire rack.

This cake is just as good, if not better, the day after it is made. To store, lightly wrap in foil and keep at room temperature. It will keep in the freezer, wrapped airtight, for up to one month.

Yield: 1 loaf-size cake

Nut & Fruit Sandwiches

    1 (16 ounce) container whipped cream cheese
    ⅓ cup good-quality lemon curd
    1½ cups finely chopped unsalted nuts (one or a combination of walnuts, pecans, hazelnuts, and almonds)
    1½ cups finely chopped dried fruit (one or a combination of any plump and moist preserved fruit: raisins, dates, figs, prunes, apricots, cherries, candied ginger, or sweetened dried cranberries)
    1½ loaves thin-sliced white bread, crusts removed

necks where the rouge stops. . . . But we must not be too hard on Sargent and complain of his bringing out the worst in people—Mama and I met Mr. Wertheimer (unfortunately without his poodle) and I must say that Sargent has positively flattered him. . . .

Affectionally,
Rose

Rose Nichols, to her sister Marian after attending the gala at London's Royal Academy for the American and British society portraitist John Singer Sargent. Rose's critical eye was drawn to two portraits: The first was the painting of the three Wyndham Sisters and the second, a nearly full-length portrait of London art patron Asher Wertheimer. Both were exhibited more recently in 1999 at the Sargent show at Boston's Museum of Fine Arts, where they received a more favorable review.

The Shaw Memorial

When exhibited at the Paris Salon in 1898, a plaster cast of Saint-Gaudens' memorial to the Civil War hero Colonel Robert Gould Shaw was the subject of some criticism—and for Rose Nichols, a vigorous defender of her uncle's work, any unfavorable review was a source of distress.

Considered one of America's finest public monuments, the sculpture honors the Massachusetts colonel who died alongside his 54th Regiment of volunteer black soldiers (popularized by the 1989 film *Glory*). In France, the memorial was largely well received—it is even said that the sculptor Auguste Rodin removed his hat as he stood before it. But it was not all praise for the sculptor, as a less generous French critic chided Saint-Gaudens for the excess of his "avenging angel" that floats above the soldiers. And back home, some

In a medium bowl, mix together cream cheese and lemon curd until combined. • Chop nuts and fruit to a medium-fine size and spread or sprinkle mixture on thin white bread that has been generously coated with cream cheese and lemon curd mixture. Top with second slice of white bread. Cut into desired size and shape.

Yield: Approximately 45

Olive, Anchovy, & Watercress Sandwiches

The following recipe is surprisingly similar to the tapenade served in the south of France.

1½ cups pitted, Mediterranean-style, green or black olives
5 anchovies packed in oil
1 tablespoon oil from anchovy tin
¾ cup tightly packed watercress (or flat parsley)
1 stick softened, unsalted butter—enough to coat bread slices
1 loaf thin-sliced bread, crusts removed

Use pitted olives if available. If not, pit olives and chop finely, using a food processor if you like. Scrape into a medium bowl and set aside. • Again using a food processor, chop watercress together with anchovies in their oil to a medium-fine consistency and thoroughly combine with olive mixture. • For each sandwich, spread softened butter on inner side of two slices of bread. • Spread a thin layer of filling on one slice of bread and cover with the second slice. Cut into three rectangles.

Yield: Approximately 48

Egg, Pimento, & Caper Sandwiches

4 large eggs, hard boiled
1 (16 ounce) container whipped cream cheese
2 tablespoons pimentos, drained and chopped
1 tablespoon small capers
1 teaspoon chopped fresh dill (the old recipe called for dill seed)
    Mayonnaise for coating bread
1 loaf thin-sliced bread, crusts removed

In a medium bowl, finely chop eggs using a fork. Add cream cheese, pimentos, capers, and dill and combine. • Coat inner sides of two slices of bread with mayonnaise and spread a thin layer of egg and cream cheese mixture on one slice of bread. Top with second slice of bread and cut into three rectangles.

Yield: Approximately 48

had grumbled that it took 14 years to complete. At one point, the exasperated head commissioner for the bronze had noted that while the memorial was still a work in progress, this was no longer true for the majority of the committee, as only 6 of the original 30 members were still alive.

Was it worth the wait? Was the angel necessary? See *A Suggested Tour* on page 122.

A Kitchen Tea

During the frigid New England
winters, with the cook at her
cast iron stove, the kitchen was
considered by many to be the
cheeriest—and warmest—room
in the Nichols House.

A
Kitchen Tea
Menu

Souffled Crackers
with clotted cream and preserves

Boiled Raisin Cake

Sponge Cake

Pecan Wafers

Graham Bread
with good homemade preserves

Irish Breakfast Tea
A Ceylon tea renowned for its hardy, strong flavor and character

A Woman in Service

A steady stream of young women had been coming to Boston from Ireland since the early 1800s seeking live-in domestic work. Although "service" work paid a higher wage, most American women shunned it as too degrading, preferring the independence of factory work. But where others had seen only degradation, the Irish woman saw opportunity. Holding her head high—some said too high—she undertook these less-valued jobs. Coming from Ireland, most often alone, she found residing and working in the better and thus safer areas of town a basic necessity. Her needs were not many: a Roman Catholic parish nearby and Irish people with whom she could continue to speak her native Gaelic.

When Mary King pressed the doorbell at 55 Mount Vernon Street one September afternoon, she was following the precedent that thousands of her fellow Irishwomen had set before her on Beacon Hill and throughout the Back Bay and South End of Boston: an interview with a potential mistress. "I still see her standing inside the door with that big hat on," Mary recalled years later. "She brought me into the parlor . . . we talked a bit and then she told me to come and live with her, that I wouldn't be sorry."

From the time Mary King arrived late in Rose Nichols' life, she worked six and one half days a week. Each day began with breakfast in bed, and lunch, previously taken out at the Parker House or the old Bellevue Hotel, was now served by Mary at home. Rose still kept to her regimen of cereal and ice cream for supper. In between, Mary attended to all the usual duties of a conscientious housekeeper. Daily chores ended at 9:30 p.m., when she brought Miss Nichols her glass of milk spiked with sherry. And for Sunday tea, store-bought cookies were soon replaced by lace cookies, delicate cakes, and "thin, thin" tea sandwiches.

Mary King remained with Rose Nichols until Miss Nichols' death, when the house became a museum under the terms of her will. Mary was asked to stay on, guiding visitors, caring for the handsome furniture, and polishing the silver tea urn until it gleamed so brightly that it was the first thing you saw when you entered the dining room. On occasion, she served up a delicious tea for special events or meetings. Mary, who had first entered 55 Mount Vernon in service, was now guardian and mistress of the fine old house.

Finally, after thirty-some years of service work in Boston, Mary retired and returned to her native Ireland. The Nichols House had been her home and her responsibility for much of her life. On departing, she was asked what it had been like working for Rose Nichols. She acknowledged that while Miss Nichols had been, perhaps, autocratic and demanding, she had also been undeniably fascinating and charismatic. Mary, as amazed as anyone over her long tenure at 55 Mount Vernon Street, added, "The first time I came here I didn't think I'd stay the week."

An American Exception

One unlikely woman in service was Bostonian Louisa May Alcott, cherished author of *Little Women*. Louisa's family was frequently in financial difficulty, often moving to different lodgings around Beacon Hill. To help make ends meet, Louisa, at age 18, briefly took a job as a live-in servant. Alcott agreed in the end with her American countrywomen, finding the experience of domestic work to be of such a demeaning nature that "every sentiment of [her] being revolted against it."

Her humbling experience is described in "How I Went Out to Service," excerpted on page 117. *A Suggested Tour*, page 122, shows the location of the Alcott homes on Pinckney Street and Louisburg Square.

Souffled Crackers

The original recipe is still remembered by many for transforming a basic common cracker into an airy frugal treat, comparable to puff pastry in appearance and texture. For whatever reason, we have had difficulty reproducing that effect so fondly remembered. After much experimentation, we have found that Vermont Common Crackers will produce a satisfactory result; second best went to ordinary saltine-type crackers. *Crackers tend to vary in puffiness. Try a few ahead of time so you know what to expect.*

    1 package Vermont Common Crackers
    1 stick unsalted butter
      Parchment paper, well greased
      Ice water
    1 ice-tray container of ice

Preheat oven to 500° F. • Cut parchment paper to fit into a large shallow-sided baking pan and grease well. • Split crackers in half (if you are using the Vermont Common Cracker) and place on parchment paper in pan. • Cover the crackers completely with cold water and ice cubes, using the ice to weigh down any of the crackers that float. Soak the crackers until they have softened, up to 4 minutes for the harder Vermont Crackers and approximately 2 minutes for the more fragile saltine-type cracker. *They must not be falling apart.* • Drain water, and if necessary, rearrange crackers in the pan. Dot each cracker with ¼ teaspoon of butter and bake 10 to 15 minutes at 500° F, until dry and puffed. Do **not** open the oven door during this time. • Reduce oven temperature to 375° F.

Continue to bake for approximately 30 minutes or until thoroughly dry and lightly browned. The crackers can be made several hours in advance and then loosely covered with foil, reheated in a 375° F oven for 3 to 5 minutes. • Serve with sweet butter and good homemade preserves.

Yield: Approximately 50

Boiled Raisin Cake

One should not be put off by the name of this recipe—although not as ethereal as the sponge cake that follows, this unusual recipe has received rave reviews.

    3 cups flour
 1¼ teaspoons baking soda
    2 cups cold water
    2 cups sugar
    3 tablespoons shortening
    1 box seedless black raisins (2½ cups)
    1 teaspoon cinnamon
    1 teaspoon nutmeg
 ½ teaspoon cloves
    1 teaspoon salt
    1 large egg, beaten
    1 cup chopped walnuts

Preheat oven to 350° F. • Into a medium bowl, sift together flour and baking soda. Set aside. • In medium saucepan, combine water, sugar, shortening, raisins, spices, and salt. Bring to a boil and lower heat to simmer. Cook, uncovered, for 5 minutes, stirring occasionally. Remove from heat, transfer to a large bowl, and cool to room temperature. • Add one-third of the flour mixture to raisin mixture and stir to combine. Beat egg and stir in. Add one-third more of the flour mixture along with walnuts. Stir to combine. Add remaining one-third and mix well. • Grease and flour two 8" x 4" loaf pans or two 6" decorative tube pans. Pour batter into pans, dividing evenly, and bake for 50 to 60 minutes. Cakes are done when a wooden skewer inserted near the center comes out clean. Cakes baked in a loaf pan will take a few minutes longer than those baked in a tube pan. • Remove pans from oven and let rest at room temperature for 10 minutes. Using a sharp knife, loosen cakes from edges of pans, and turn out onto wire racks to cool completely. This cake will keep at room temperature, well-wrapped, for up to three days. For longer storage, wrap airtight and freeze for up to one month.

Yield: Two 8"x by 4" loaves or two 6" decorative tube cakes

Sponge Cake

Sponge cake, together with angel food and chiffon cakes, forms one of the mainstays of the tea table. In fact, it is one of most useful categories of cake recipes to master. The large quantity of egg yolks and beaten egg whites give sponge cake its fine texture. This cake may be thinly sliced and filled as a sandwich with any fruit and nut spread, softened whipped cream cheese, or a combination of both. This cake recipe, if baked in a low and wide rectangular pan, will produce an excellent cake to roll up, using any filling of your choice. However, you will have to reduce the cooking time. This recipe produces a fine, moist cake that is easy to make.

1⅓ cups sifted cake flour
½ teaspoon baking powder
½ teaspoon salt
1½ cups sugar
6 large eggs, separated
½ cup water
1 teaspoon vanilla
1 teaspoon lemon juice
1 teaspoon cream of tartar

Preheat oven to 375° F. • In a large bowl, sift together the flour, baking powder, salt, and one cup of sugar. Set aside. • In a medium bowl, combine the egg yolks, water, vanilla, and lemon juice. Beat lightly with a whisk. • Add the egg-yolk mixture to the sifted dry ingredients and whisk until the mixture is thoroughly combined. • In a large mixing bowl beat the egg whites with an electric beater until foamy. Add the cream of tartar and continue to beat at medium-high speed until soft peaks are formed. Gradually add the remaining ½ cup sugar, beating at high speed if using a hand

Tea at the Athenaeum

Rose Nichols, like many Bostonians, was a member of the Boston Athenaeum. For years, afternoon tea was served in the august surroundings of this private library, located on the crest of Beacon Hill. Readers joined the staff daily to take tea with crackers (one sweet and one plain) for three cents. The teas were suspended in 1959 when the director overheard some of those gathered referring to the Athenaeum as "that Athenian tea room" and decided right then and there that "it was a good time to make books the only refreshment offered to our readers." Fortunately for today's members and their guests, the tradition has been revived, with a more elaborate tea menu—and correspondingly higher price.

See *A Suggested Tour* on page 122. For information on guided tours, telephone the Athenaeum at 617-227-0270.

mixer, or at medium-high when using a standing mixer. Beat until stiff peaks are formed. • Add a quarter of the egg whites to the egg-yolk-flour mixture, and whisk gently to combine. This will lighten the mixture and make it easier to fold in the remaining egg whites. Add the remaining whites and fold in gently and quickly until they are incorporated. • Pour batter into an ungreased 10″ tube pan and bake for about 35 minutes. The top will be golden brown and will spring back when lightly touched. Remove from oven and invert pan by placing the center tube opening over a thin-necked bottle. (A wine or whiskey bottle neck should do.) Let the cake remain in this position until it is completely cool. Using a flexible thin-bladed knife, release the cake around the sides of the tube pan, and then from the bottom of the pan. The cake may be stored, loosely wrapped with foil, at room temperature for two days. It will keep frozen, wrapped airtight, for up to one month.

Yield: One 10″ tube cake

Pecan Wafers

The pecan, known as the American nut, is at its best when freshly roasted. Be demanding about freshness in nuts, and never use previously opened packages, unless they have been stored in the refrigerator or freezer.

⅓ cup sugar
½ cup softened, unsalted butter
 1 large egg
¼ cup flour
½ cup toasted finely chopped or ground pecans
    About 30 unsalted pecan halves

Preheat oven to 350° F. • In a medium bowl, using an electric mixer, cream together the sugar and butter until light and fluffy. Add egg and keep beating, scraping down bowl as needed. Continue to beat until fluffy. • Sift in flour and add the finely chopped pecans. Stir to combine. • Onto greased cookie sheet, drop batter by scant teaspoons, leaving room for wafers to spread. Top each with a pecan half, and bake for 8 to 10 minutes or until wafers have just begun to brown lightly at edges. Remove wafers from oven and cool on wire rack. Store at room temperature in an airtight container, with waxed paper between layers for up to one week. Freeze, wrapped airtight, for up to one month.

Yield: Approximately 30

Graham Bread

This bread is both delicious and simple to make. It stands alone on its own merit. Serve it toasted for breakfast as well as for tea.

3 cups whole wheat flour
½ cup white flour
1 tablespoon baking powder
1 teaspoon baking soda
1 teaspoon salt
3 tablespoons melted butter
1½ cups buttermilk
½ cup molasses
½ cup chopped unsalted walnuts (or pecans, if you prefer)

Preheat oven to 350° F. • Into a large bowl, sift wheat and white flour together with baking powder, baking soda, and salt. Set aside. • In a separate bowl, add melted shortening, buttermilk, and molasses. Stir to combine. • Add liquid mixture to flour mixture and stir just enough to combine. Fold in chopped nuts. • Pour batter into a greased 9" x 5" loaf pan. Bake 45 to 50 minutes, or until a wooden skewer inserted in the center of the loaf comes out clean. Let bread cool in pan and then remove. • If you are making tea sandwiches, thinly slice the bread, spread the filling, and cut into desired shapes. Wrapped tightly in plastic, this bread keeps well at room temperature. It may also be frozen.

Yield: Approximately 40

A Kitchen Tea

If you are fortunate enough to have a pleasant and roomy kitchen, why not hold an informal tea party there? As many discovered at the Nichols House, the kitchen, with its irresistible aromas and warmth, was the most cheerful spot. If you have confidence in your baking ability, consider serving right from the oven. Now is the time to use your less formal teaware—the intimacy of the kitchen will no doubt bring a congeniality not easily found in a more formal setting.

Tea in Bed

"Proper Boston women, it
was said, liked getting old.
Abolitionist Julia Ward Howe,
who wrote 'The Battle Hymn
of the Republic' and lived to
be ninety-one, believed that
aging was like a cup of tea:
the sugar was at the bottom."

—*The Nature of Massachusetts*, 1996

Tea in Bed
Menu

Fine Little Cakes

Butterscotch Oatmeal Cookies

Orange Bread

Scrambled Eggs & Smoked Salmon Sandwiches

Eggnog with a Dash of Sherry (optional)

Darjeeling Tea

The champagne of teas, with a fine muscatel fragrance

Nothing quite compares to the pleasure of being served tea in bed. This morning ritual provides the chance to collect oneself before plunging headlong into the day.

For Rose Nichols, this delightful habit began each morning at precisely 8:15 when Mary King would carry a breakfast tray of freshly squeezed orange juice, a pot of steaming tea, and a dropped egg on toast up winding flights of stairs to serve Miss Nichols in her handsome, leaf-green bedroom. Alas, most of us do not have someone in our service to help us greet the morning in such an agreeable way. Still breakfast in bed is a pleasure in which we ought to indulge from time to time.

Of course, tea in bed need not be designated solely as a breakfast event— after all, Colette, the hale and steamy French novelist, worked from her bed and took meals and tea there, as did the ailing Robert Louis Stevenson. In fact, Stevenson's good friend, and Rose's uncle, Augustus Saint-Gaudens, portrayed the author in bed in two versions of a commemorative bronze plaque. In the first, he holds a lit cigarette; in the second, the cigarette has been replaced by a pen—more suitable in a depiction of the young writer who was dying of consumption.

"Promptly at ten o'clock every day Miss Nichols had her eggnog with a nice bit of sherry in it. Lunch was at one, another eggnog came at three o'clock and dinner— supper really—was about six-thirty."

Mary King

Fine Little Cakes

While you may frost these dainty little cakes, we prefer serving them plain. The combination of mace and coriander gives them an appealing flavor and aroma. (Use only recently purchased spices for this recipe.)

2 sticks softened, unsalted butter
¾ cup sugar
2 cups flour
1 teaspoon ground mace
½ teaspoon ground coriander
3 large eggs, separated
1 cup currants

Preheat oven to 350° F. • In a large bowl, use an electric beater to cream butter and sugar until light and fluffy. • Combine flour, mace, and coriander, sift over creamed mixture, and blend. Beat egg yolks, one at a time, into the batter. • In a medium bowl, beat egg whites until soft peaks form, then fold into batter. Add currants and stir to distribute evenly. • Grease mini-muffin pans and dust with flour. Fill three-quarters full with batter. Bake 15 to 20 minutes, or until a wooden skewer inserted in the center comes out clean. Remove from oven and let cool for 5 minutes. Remove cakes from pans to cool completely on a wire rack. These little cakes may be made up to 48 hours in advance and kept in an airtight tin at room temperature. They may also be frozen for up to one month.

Yield: 48

Butterscotch Oatmeal Cookies

Tea on a Tray

Our suggestions for the tea tray follow those given by Fannie Merritt Farmer many years ago in *The Boston Cooking School Cookbook*: It is best to use a sturdy but lightweight, footed tray, covered with a linen cloth or placemat. The tray should be large enough to accommodate warm serving dishes, the necessary utensils, and a small pot of tea. An attractive thermos jug may also be used to keep the tea warm, or, as an alternative, a pretty tea cozy. A tiny vase with a miniature bouquet of flowers along with the daily newspaper would be thoughtful. Finally, if you have overnight guests from out of town, why not provide a map and a tour book of places you know will be of interest to them. By serving breakfast on a tray, you give your guests great comfort, and yourself time for your own morning's affairs.

These cookies are a later addition to Mary King's recipe collection, but hold up well to her deserved reputation for delicate, light treats.

 6 ounces butterscotch bits (about 1 cup)
 1 stick unsalted butter
 1 large egg
 1 cup quick-cooking rolled oats
 ½ cup sifted flour
 1 teaspoon baking powder
 ¼ teaspoon salt

Preheat oven to 300° F. • Melt butterscotch bits in top of a double boiler over low heat. When melted, remove from heat and blend in butter with a fork. Let cool to lukewarm, and beat in egg using fork or whisk. • Combine the remaining dry ingredients and add to the butterscotch mixture. • Drop by half teaspoons onto an ungreased cookie sheet. Bake for 10 to 12 minutes. Using a thin-bladed spatula, immediately remove from cookie sheet and cool on rack. • Store in an airtight container, placing waxed paper between layers. These cookies may be made up to 48 hours in advance.

To store, freeze in an airtight container for up to one month.

Yield: Approximately 60

Orange Bread

1 stick softened, unsalted butter
1 cup sugar
2 cups flour, sifted
1 teaspoon baking soda
¼ teaspoon salt
2 large eggs, lightly beaten
    Juice of 2 large oranges with their grated zest (approximately
    2 tablespoons)
1 cup raisins

Preheat oven to 350° F. • In a large mixing bowl, cream butter and sugar until mixture is light and fluffy. • Combine flour, baking soda, and salt in sifter and sift over creamed butter mixture. Add remaining ingredients, blend well. • Pour batter into a greased 9" x 5" loaf pan. Bake for approximately 40 minutes, or until a wooden skewer inserted into the middle of cake comes out clean. • Cool on a wire rack, right side up. When completely cooled, wrap tightly in heavy foil. Freeze, wrapped airtight, for up to three months.

Yield: Approximately 24 slices

Fannie Merritt Farmer

Boston was fortunate in having its very own equivalent to Isabella Beeton and Constance Spry, England's doyennes of home management and cookery, in Miss Fannie Merritt Farmer. While a student at The Boston Cooking School, she published the instantly successful *The Boston Cooking School Cookbook* in 1896. Like its English counterparts, her cookbook also contained invaluable information on running a household, and no young bride would be without her Fannie Farmer's.

As director of The Boston Cooking School, Fanny Farmer is credited with introducing spoon and cup measurements, replacing the heretofore inaccurate "pinch" and "size of walnut" directions.

Scrambled Eggs &
Smoked Salmon Sandwiches

Author's family recipe

Although less dainty than thin white bread, we recommend using the graham bread recipe found on page 67 for this sandwich—it will be more substantial and hold up better with the filling.

> 1 dozen large eggs
>   Spray oil for coating pan, or a non-stick skillet
> 12 ounces smoked salmon
> 2 tablespoons good horseradish sauce (obtainable at most markets)
> 3 tablespoons chopped fresh dill
> 1½ sticks unsalted butter, softened

Using a non-stick skillet, or a skillet sprayed lightly with oil, scramble eggs until well done, but still moist. • Chop into small pieces to make a textured mixture. Do not puree. • Chop the smoked salmon into a fine or medium mince. Add dill and horseradish sauce (not regular horseradish) and mix thoroughly. • Spread softened butter on the inner side of each slice of graham bread. • Spread on a layer of salmon mixture. Spoon a layer of egg mixture on top and cover with a buttered slice of bread. Cut into desired shapes.

Yield: Approximately 40

Eggnog with a Dash of Sherry

  1 egg, beaten slightly (if you have any concern about
      salmonella, you may substitute a pasteurized egg product)
  1 tablespoon sugar
    Pinch of salt
  ⅔ cup cold whole milk
  1½ tablespoons sherry
    Nutmeg for grating

Using a wire whisk, beat egg with sugar and salt until very light.
Add milk and sherry, beating constantly. Strain into glass and
grate nutmeg over top.

Yield: 1 serving

The Collection

Over the years, Rose Nichols acquired several important sculptures by her uncle Augustus Saint-Gaudens. One, a bronze of the goddess Diana, is a 21-inch version of the weather vane Saint-Gaudens created for his friend and collaborator, the architect Stanford White, to crown the new Madison Square Garden in New York City. The original gilded Diana graced the building from 1893 until it was razed in 1925. A second work by Saint-Gaudens is the Robert Louis Stevenson plaque (see page 76), and a third, the head of the "Winged Victory," or "Nike," taken from the monumental bronze statue of General W. T. Sherman. Saint-Gaudens was an early advocate of artists augmenting their incomes by making reductions of their work in limited editions. He was known to be generous with these works, often giving them to family members—and Rose was a favorite. But she also earned these gifts by serving as her uncle's sales agent for a time, negotiating contracts on his behalf with Tiffany & Company and several other fine establishments.

A Christmas Tea

"The tea party is a most charming custom, which could make a celebrated return during the holiday season, when so many events are at such a 'high pitch.' A good tea offers a distinctly pleasurable event—and most importantly, it is a custom both the old and the very young can enjoy together."

—*The Constance Spry Cookery Book*, 1956

A Christmas Tea Menu

Lace Cookies

Special Fruitcake

Orange Glazed Walnut Squares

Ham & Cheese Puffs

Shrimp Sandwiches

Spinach Squares

Chicken Salad on Graham Bread

Orange Chiffon Cake

Nichols House Rum Cakes

Bell Ringers' Eggnog

Ginger Frappé

Candied Grapefruit Peel

Yunnan Tea

*A venerable tea dating back nearly 2000 years and known for its hint of mocha—
unlike most China tea, it is robust enough to tolerate a dash of milk*

Decorations
Candied Mint Leaves
Inedible Frosted Holly Leaves
Inedible Decorative Leaves
Sugared Rose

"*Beacon Hill,*" *Miss Rose's sister Margaret wrote in her memoir,* Lively Days, *"is said to be the first locality in the United States to celebrate Christmas by illuminating windows on Christmas Eve. . . . My husband's younger brother Alfred originated the practice by placing a burning candle in the fourth-floor window of his home at 9 West Cedar Street in 1893." And by 1908, Margaret recounted, this custom had spread throughout the Hill.*

The Nichols family kept Christmas in the proper Beacon Hill fashion, hosting holiday teas for as many as fifty guests. The following recipes represent those dishes that one might have expected to find on their Christmas tea table.

"*On the ground floor, curtains were drawn aside and each window was decorated with special care. A Madonna, perhaps a small bas-relief or a decorative fruit arrangement, was illuminated by a pair of handsome brass candles. The little back alleys were just as much fun to visit as Mount Vernon or West Cedar Streets. My father's house, which faced [down the hill] had at least one candle in each window. . . . The large square Sears house at 85 Mount Vernon Street . . . was a special attraction, with its display of one hundred and ten candles in its fifteen windows, including the lookout on top of the house. No doubt the custom created a fire hazard, but individual charm beamed out of every window. Singers wandered around in a haphazard manner and crowds were anxious not to miss a window or a chorus. The simplicity and beauty of the surroundings inspired a new kind of Christmas spirit.*"

Lace Cookies

You will find these delicately thin and crispy cookies easy to make. But remember that all lace cookies need lots of space to spread out while baking.

⅔ cup packed brown sugar
1 stick softened, unsalted butter
2 tablespoons flour
2 tablespoons milk
1 teaspoon vanilla
1¼ cups old fashioned rolled oats

Preheat oven to 350° F. • In a medium mixing bowl, cream sugar and butter together until light and fluffy. Sprinkle flour over mixture and beat just to incorporate. Beat in milk and vanilla. Stir in oats. • Grease and dust a large cookie sheet with flour. • Drop batter by half teaspoons onto cookie sheet. The cookies will spread almost three inches, so leave adequate space. Bake for 10 minutes, or until the cookies are browned around the edges and the centers have a lacy pattern. Remove from oven and let rest for a minute or two. The cookies need to firm enough for easy removal, but do not wait too long, or they will stick to the pan. Cool on wire rack. • Cookies can be made up to 24 hours in advance, and will keep in an airtight container in a dry, cool place. The cookies can be re-crisped in a 350° F oven for 5 minutes. Do not freeze.

Yield: Approximately 50

Special Fruitcake

Author's family recipe

The ingredients make this a very expensive recipe. It freezes well, however, and people will be happy to eat this fruitcake in June! The following recipe will make approximately 12 small loaf cakes using 5¾" x 3¼" x 2" pans or 5 large loaves, using 8" x 3¾" x 2½" size pans.

6 cups unsalted pecans
6 cups unsalted walnuts
32 ounces pitted dates
2 cups seeded raisins (you may substitute ½ cup candied ginger or dried cranberries)
3 cups marinated, drained and pitted maraschino cherries
1⅓ cups diced orange peels, cooked in water (or steamed) until softened, all white pith removed (keep the pieces large— it will be easier to remove pith and dice the peel after it has softened)
3 cups flour
2 teaspoons baking powder
½ teaspoon salt
3 cups sugar
1 dozen large eggs
2 tablespoons good brandy

Optional (but highly recommended) Brandy or Rum Syrup:
1 stick unsalted butter
½ cup dark rum or good brandy

Preheat oven to 300° F. • In a very large bowl, combine nuts and fruit. Combine flour, baking powder, and salt, and sift over fruit and nuts. Thoroughly mix fruit and flour mixtures together using your hands. • In a separate bowl, beat eggs and sugar until light and fluffy, add brandy and pour over the fruit and nuts. Mix until completely blended. *We use our hands to simplify this procedure—you may wear plastic gloves if you like.* • Using a large spoon, fill disposable aluminum loaf pans, firmly pressing mixture down. Note: Leave some of the liquid batter to drizzle over each fruitcake. • Bake for approximately 2 hours and 30 minutes for the large loaves and 1 hour and 30 minutes for the small loaves. Remove from oven. • While the fruitcakes are still warm, make a syrup by melting a stick of butter in ½ cup of brandy or rum. Stir to combine and pour 1 to 2 tablespoons of syrup over the cakes. • Let fruitcakes cool in pans. Wrap tightly in heavy aluminum foil and store in refrigerator until ready to serve. They will keep for two weeks. Thinly slice in the aluminum pans and serve. Tightly wrapped in heavy foil, these fruitcakes have been successfully frozen for six months.

Yield: 12 small or 5 large loaves

Orange Glazed Walnut Squares

1 stick unsalted butter
1 cup unsifted flour
1 teaspoon granulated sugar

The Rt. Reverend Phillips Brooks

It is not widely known that Boston's distinguished Episcopal bishop, the Rt. Reverend Phillips Brooks (1835-1893) was also the author of the popular Christmas carol, "O Little Town of Bethlehem." A statue of Brooks by Augustus Saint-Gaudens stands on the Boylston Street side of Trinity Church in Boston's Back Bay.

See *A Suggested Tour,* page 122.

⅛ teaspoon salt
2 large eggs
1 cup light brown sugar
½ teaspoon baking powder
1 teaspoon vanilla
½ cup coarsely chopped unsalted walnuts

Glaze:
1 cup powdered sugar
2 tablespoons thawed orange juice concentrate

Preheat oven to 350° F. • Melt butter in a 9" square baking pan in preheated oven. Set aside but keep warm. Note: a 12" square pan will make a thinner bottom crust and a more delicate square. • In a small bowl stir to combine flour, sugar, and salt. • Stir flour mixture into warm, melted butter in the baking pan until a dough is formed. Cool. • Place a piece of plastic wrap over the dough (the plastic should be larger than the pan). Using your fingers, spread the dough out evenly in pan. • Bake 10 minutes. Set aside. • In a medium bowl, beat eggs with an electric beater until frothy. Beat in brown sugar, baking powder, and vanilla. Stir in nuts and pour over baked crust. Bake 20 to 25 minutes. Set aside and cool for approximately 10 to 15 minutes.

Glaze: In a small bowl, mix enough orange juice concentrate with powdered sugar to make a glaze that can be easily spread over the baked filling. Allow to cool completely before cutting into small, dainty squares.

These squares will keep well in an airtight tin for two weeks.

Yield: Approximately 50

Ham & Cheese Puffs

These puffs are at their best served warm—straight from the oven. We would discourage serving them any other way. But to get these tasty bites to the tea table before they cool, you will need assistance in preparation.

Batter (Pâte à Choux):
1 cup beer
1 stick unsalted butter, cut into pieces
¼ teaspoon salt
1 cup sifted flour
4 large eggs
2 cups ground ham
1 cup grated Gruyere cheese
3 tablespoons Dijon mustard
3 tablespoons grated Parmesan cheese
   Salt and pepper

Egg Wash:
1 large egg
1 tablespoon water

A Passion for Bells

Arthur Howard Nichols' birth in 1840 in the shadow of Boston's Old North Church steeple may well have led to his lifelong fascination with bells. By the age of 12, Rose's father was regularly ringing at "Old North," with a repertoire that ranged from hymns to the popular ditty, "Oh, Dear! What Can the Matter Be?" So avid was his lifelong passion that, in 1910, he traveled to Washington, D.C., in a heartfelt but unsuccessful attempt to convince Congress that the soon-to-be-built tower above Boston's U.S. Customs House would not be complete without bells. The problem with bells, it seems, is that while people think them a splendid idea, in the end no one wishes to live near such clamor.

Preheat oven to 425° F. • In a medium-size, heavy saucepan, bring beer, butter, and salt to a boil over high heat. Reduce heat to low. Add sifted flour all at once, beating mixture with a wooden spoon until it leaves the sides of the saucepan and forms a ball. • Transfer dough to the bowl of an electric mixer. With the mixer on high speed, beat in the eggs, one at a time, beating well after each addition. The batter should be thick enough to hold soft peaks. If it becomes too stiff, beat an additional egg lightly in a small bowl and add enough egg to thin the batter. Fold in ham, Gruyere, mustard, and Parmesan. Add salt and pepper to taste. • Transfer mixture to a pastry bag fitted with ½-inch plain tip and pipe 1-inch puffs 1 inch apart on a buttered baking sheet. For a more handmade appearance, you may also drop mixture by teaspoon onto a buttered baking sheet. • Brush top of each puff with an egg wash made by lightly beating 1 egg with 1 tablespoon water. *Note*: be careful not to let egg wash drip onto baking sheet, or it may prevent the puff's rising. • Bake 10 minutes in preheated oven, and then reduce temperature to 400° F, baking the puffs for approximately 15 minutes more. Remove from oven, and, with a sharp knife, cut a small slit into the side of each puff to allow any steam to escape and bake 5 minutes more. Serve puffs warm from the oven.

Yield: 60 to 70

The Heir Apparent

Seeking someone to share his passion for bells, Dr. Nichols turned to Rose's youngest sister Margaret. Learning to handle a tower bell at Boston's Church of the Advent during the hot summer of 1900, Margaret described herself as "the only woman present, often disheveled and woefully out of place, having for months of practice never having heard [her] bell," for as a beginner, her clapper had been tied.

Shrimp Sandwiches

½ pound shrimp, cooked, shelled, and deveined
1 stick unsalted butter, softened and cut into small pieces
2 tablespoons heavy cream
1 tablespoon lemon juice
2 teaspoons tomato paste
1 teaspoon anchovy paste
1 stick softened, unsalted butter for coating bread slices
1½ loaves thin-sliced bread, crusts removed

In a food processor combine all ingredients and puree until smooth. • Coat inner sides of bread with softened butter. • Spread filling on buttered bread and top with slice of buttered bread. Cut into three rectangles.

Yield: Approximately 60

Margaret went on to master this strenuous art, earning respect at home and abroad for her skill. Marriage and six children put an end to Margaret's tower ringing, but she did establish the Beacon Hill tradition of handbell ringing on Christmas Eve, when she and her family troupe performed for neighbors—a tradition that continues to this day. Margaret's last peal from a tower was at her father's memorial. And it is thought that her last handringing was at the end of World War II, when she proclaimed this joyous event by running through the Boston Common ringing her bells!

Spinach Squares

These tasty morsels can be served hot or at room temperature.

3 small onions
3 tablespoons unsalted butter
4 large eggs, beaten
1½ cups milk
1½ cups flour
1½ teaspoons salt
1½ teaspoons baking powder

1½ pounds sharp cheddar cheese, grated
2 pounds fresh spinach, cooked, drained, and chopped,
or two 10-ounce packages of frozen chopped spinach,
cooked, with excess water squeezed out

Preheat oven to 350° F. • Finely chop onions. (Although the original recipe did not include this direction, you may want to sauté the onions until translucent.) • Place butter into a 15" x 11½" baking pan to melt in preheated oven. Remove pan from oven and spread butter to evenly coat bottom of pan. Reserve any excess butter and set pan aside. • In a large bowl, combine beaten eggs and milk. Combine flour, salt, and baking powder and sift over the beaten eggs, beating until thoroughly blended. Add grated cheese, spinach, and onion. Add the reserved melted butter and mix well. • Spread mixture evenly in buttered pan. Bake for 30 minutes, or until mixture is firm to the touch and beginning to brown at the edges. • Remove from oven and let cool in pan. Cut into small squares. If sealed in an airtight container, these squares may be refrigerated for 48 hours, then reheated in a 350° F oven until hot. They may also be frozen for up to three weeks, brought to room temperature, and reheated.

Yield: Approximately 75

Savouries

Not all tea food is sweet. In Victorian Britain many tea table offerings were called savouries —food more akin to hors d'oeuvres. This type of food is best complemented by a strong, full-bodied tea.

Chicken Salad on Graham Bread

Rose's mother, Elizabeth Nichols, served these sandwiches at her well-attended Christmas tea on December 18, 1893.

Chicken Salad:
6-8 pound capon or fowl (any stewing chicken may be used)
    Mayonnaise (if store-bought, add a little fresh lemon juice)
1½ cups of chopped flat-leaf parsley
    Salt and pepper to taste

Graham Bread: see page 67

Preheat oven to 350° F. • Simmer stewing chicken in a large pot until tender. The length of time needed for cooking will vary according to the size and age of the bird; follow the directions found in any cookbook. Let the bird cool completely. Remove the skin and discard all but the cleanest pieces of meat, preferably using the white meat only and reserving the remainder for another use. • Finely chop the meat. Do not puree, as the filling should have texture. • Add enough mayonnaise to the chopped chicken to make it easy to spread. Add parsley and season with salt and pepper to taste. The chicken salad should be stored tightly covered and may be made a day or two in advance.

A Frugal Thought: Strain and keep the liquid from the stewing bird. By placing the broth in the refrigerator overnight, the fat will congeal, making it easy to remove and discard. You will be left with an excellent chicken broth for a later use.

Yield: Approximately 40

Capon or Fowl

In years past, it was easy to find these tasty stewing birds. Both the capon—a castrated young rooster—and the fowl—the old meaty hen—have now become culinary luxuries.

Orange Chiffon Cake

1 cup plus 2 tablespoons sifted cake flour
1½ teaspoons baking powder
½ teaspoon salt
¾ cup sugar
¼ cup vegetable oil
2 large eggs, separated
  Grated zest of 1 orange (about 1½ tablespoons)
⅜ cup orange juice
¼ teaspoon cream of tartar

Preheat oven to 325° F. • Sift flour, baking powder, and salt into a large bowl. Add sugar. Make a hole in the dry mixture and, using an electric mixer, beat in remaining ingredients in the following order: vegetable oil, egg yolks, orange zest, and orange juice. Beat until smooth. Set aside. • In a separate bowl, combine egg whites and cream of tartar, and beat until stiff. Do *not* underbeat. • Gradually pour egg-yolk mixture over beaten egg whites, and using a rubber scraper, gently fold in until blended. Do *not* stir. • Pour into ungreased 10″ tube pan and bake for 50 to 55 minutes.

Yield: Approximately 35 thin slices

Nichols House Rum Cakes

Nothing could be simpler or more intoxicatingly delicious than this rum cake. A shallow baking pan will assure that the rum syrup thoroughly penetrates the cake, while a bundt or ring pan will absorb the syrup on the bottom only.

1 package good yellow cake mix (we used Duncan Hines)
1 cup water added to the cake mix
1 package vanilla pudding mix (we used Jello brand)
4 large eggs
½ cup solid vegetable oil (Crisco)
½ cup dark rum

Preheat oven to 325° F. • In a large bowl, use an electric mixer to beat the above ingredients in the order in which they are listed, thoroughly beating in each addition until the batter is blended. • Pour batter in to a 15" x 11" x 1½" baking pan. Bake for 30 minutes, or until a wooden skewer inserted into the center of the cake comes out dry.

Syrup:
1 stick unsalted butter
1 cup sugar
1 cup water
¼ cup dark rum

In a medium saucepan, melt butter and add sugar, stirring to mix thoroughly. Add water and bring to boil, stirring until all ingredients are incorporated. Remove from stove. Stir in rum. • Spoon syrup over hot cake until it does not absorb any more liquid. Cover and "cure" for ten days. To serve, cut into small squares.

Yield: Approximately 65

A Word About Eggs

Some of us remember when grocers provided egg illuminators, on which each egg was placed to inspect for clarity and freshness before it was sold. Even earlier, in 1861, Mrs. Beeton, the English authority on household management, suggested, "In choosing eggs, apply the tongue to the large end of the egg, and if it feels warm, it is new and may be relied on as a fresh egg."

Nowadays such intimacy with the egg is no longer required as modern egg cartons customarily bear "sell by" dates. However, if you have been harboring eggs for an uncertain length of time, we advise following Mrs. Beeton's sage advice: Eggs that cannot be relied on should always be broken in a separate cup. By taking this simple precaution, you will avoid tainting your cooking with a bad egg.

Bell Ringers' Eggnog

It is a fine Scottish tradition to hold a formal tea during the Christmas holidays. There is nothing quite so over-the-top as the following eggnog. With the exception of Christmas or New Year's, you would not normally serve alcohol at a tea party. If you have doubt about the quality or freshness of eggs available to you, most stores now offer pasturized eggs, which may be used as a substitute.

1 dozen large eggs, separated
1 box powdered sugar
1 quart milk
1 quart cream
1 quart bourbon
1 pint rum
1 pint brandy

Beat egg yolks well and add sugar, milk, and cream. Stir in liquor. Beat egg whites separately and add to top. Sprinkle with freshly grated nutmeg and serve. This recipe may be doubled.

Yield: Approximately 30 punch cups

Ginger Frappé

½ pound chopped fresh ginger (you may use an electric mincer)
1 cup sugar
1 quart cold water

½ cup fresh orange juice
½ cup fresh lemon juice
1 pint freshly brewed China tea (not Hu-Kwa)
Cheesecloth

Chop ginger and place it into a medium-sized, heavy-bottomed saucepan. Add sugar and water. Boil for 15 minutes, watching carefully, and add fruit juices and tea. Set aside to cool. • Strain and squeeze through washed cheesecloth. • Pour over crushed ice, which has been placed in a chilled punch bowl. Serve immediately.

Yield: Approximately 12 punch cups. This recipe may be doubled.

Candied Grapefruit Peel

Author's family recipe

3 grapefruit
3 cups sugar
1½ cups water

Eat three grapefruit and reserve the peel. Remove white pith and cut peel into 1" to 2" strips. Place peel in a large heavy-bottomed pot and cover with water. Bring to a boil and simmer for 10 minutes. Drain and repeat two or three times, or until soft, then drain

Decorative Ice Block for the Punch Bowl

It is a good idea to use block ice for frappés or punches, as small cubes will quickly melt and water down your punch. For a pretty effect, try making a decorated ice block:

Half fill a metal ring pan with water and freeze until nearly set. Decorate with a wreath of candied fruit and mint leaves or with a spray of edible flowers. Gently press the fruit and leaves or flowers into the soft ice. Refreeze. When frozen add enough water to fill the pan and return to freezer until solidly frozen.

again, and remove peel. • Put 3 cups sugar and 1½ cups water in the same pot. Cook over a medium heat, stirring until sugar dissolves. Add peel and cook, watching carefully and turning the peel over from time to time until most of the syrup is absorbed (about 25 minutes). • One by one, lay the peel out to dry on waxed paper. Leave for 12 hours or overnight. Roll each peel in granulated sugar and layer them in an airtight container, placing waxed paper between layers. • Grapefruit peel may also be frozen or stored in tightly sealed plastic bags. They are delicious served after dinner with coffee as well as at tea.

Yield: Approximately 6 cups

Candied Mint Leaves

Author's family recipe

Candied mint leaves make a tasty bite, served separately or used to garnish dishes on a table. Powered egg whites should be used to avoid any problem with bacteria.

Fresh mint leaves—as many as needed
Powdered egg whites (We used the brand Just Whites, but any brand, available at most supermarkets, will do.)
Powdered sugar

Wash fresh mint leaves and dry gently with paper towels. Keeping whole, dip them into a bowl containing reconstituted egg white. • Using a sifter, cover leaves with powdered sugar, making certain that both sides are well coated. Shake off excess sugar. • Place leaves on tray and allow to harden in the refrigerator. Store the leaves in an airtight container between sheets of waxed paper. They should keep for a week in a dry, cool location.

Inedible Frosted Holly Leaves

Fresh holly sprigs that have been frosted with powdered sugar are the perfect decorating accent for a Christmas tea. The following is a very old recipe from *Beeton's Book of Household Management*.

Sprigs of holly
Clarified butter (the liquid part only)
Superfine granulated sugar

Procure some nice sprigs of holly; pick the leaves from the stalks, and wipe them with a clean cloth to remove all moisture. • Place the holly near the fire (or in a barely warm oven) to thoroughly dry, but do not shrivel the leaves! Dip them into the melted butter, and sprinkle some sugar over them. • Dry them in a warm spot. They should be kept in a dry place, as any damp would spoil their appearance.

December 19, 1893

Dear Rose,

My [Christmas] tea yesterday was very successful. It was a fine day and I think there were fifty here. Aunt Genie was head of the tea department and was assisted by four others. . . . I ordered some pink primroses and cut flowers and Mr. Parkman sent two dozen beautiful roses. . . . Then we had a little mistletoe scattered about to give a sort of Christmas effect and the rooms looked very attractive. . . . There were enough men to make a fair showing. . . . The ladies began to come punctually at four to my great surprise and some of them stayed fully an hour. . . . We had a table in the parlor with one 'frappé' . . . [and] graham bread, chicken and lettuce sandwiches, with tea and chocolate in the dining room."
—*E. F. X.*

Elizabeth Nichols, to her daughter Rose

Inedible Decorative Leaves

Author's family recipe

Magnolia leaves are best, but laurel, holly, and similar leaves may be treated in the same manner. The leaves should be green and full grown. To "skeletonize" leaves, place them in a large saucepan with a handful of baking soda, and cover with water. Bring to a boil and simmer for an hour or so. Remove the leaves from the water and scrape away the softened tissue, leaving the veins exposed. Wash in clear water and dry between blotting paper or paper towels. If you want light-colored veins, place in a bowl and cover with a solution of domestic bleach, leaving for several hours or overnight and rinse thoroughly and dry.

Sugared Rose

Author's family recipe

Miss Rose would most certainly have approved of these little delicacies, the rose never being too far from hand. Her "signature" flower appears often in her needlework and her china, as may be observed throughout the Nichols House Museum.

    2 teaspoons powdered egg whites
    2 tablespoons warm water
    ¾ cup superfine granulated sugar
    1 fresh rose, free of pesticides

Combine powdered egg whites and water in a small bowl. •
Place sugar in another small bowl, and set aside. • Gently remove
the petals from your selected rose. Coat each petal with egg-white
mixture using a small soft brush. • Dip petal in sugar mixture to
coat and gently transfer to rack. • Thoroughly dry petals at room
temperature for approximately 6 to 8 hours. • To reassemble the
rose, place the larger outside petals on a serving dish. Continue
layering the medium-sized petals, followed by the small center
petals, until you have formed a rose. To store loose petals prior to
assembling, place petals in layers between paper towels in an
airtight container at room temperature. The petals will keep for
approximately two weeks.

Yield: 1 reconstructed rose

"China tea offered plain or with thin slices of lemon is the only way the connoisseur will accept his tea—anything else used to flavor such a delicate beverage is barbaric."

—*The Constance Spry Cookery Book*, 1956

Part Three

Planning and Preparing a Tea Party

If you are having tea with family, or with a friend, it is difficult to outdo the simplicity of an old-fashioned tea favorite such as cinnamon toast—warm, thin buttered toast sprinkled with a mixture of cinnamon and superfine sugar—always perfect with any tea. When planning a grand tea event, read on, but be advised that Miss Rose, toward the end of her tea party hosting, decided against serving any food at all—talk was to triumph over palate.

Tea

When planning a tea party, your first task is to evaluate your guests to determine what type of tea to serve. Traditionally, Bostonians have favored smoky teas, such as Lapsang Souchong or Hu-Kwa. Much like the Boston hat or Miss Nichols' opinions on world affairs, a cup of Hu-Kwa is sturdy, strong, and full of personality. Not everyone, however, cares for such a strong, smoky flavor. If you are not certain of your guests' tastes, you might begin with a milder tea or a blend—perhaps Darjeeling, Assam, China Oolong, or, really, any tea deemed an "afternoon tea." Serious tea drinkers tend toward strong tea, but if you have hot water and milk at hand to dilute the tea for those less committed drinkers, everyone should feel well attended.

There are probably as many types of tea as there are teapots. The true connoisseur keeps a teapot for each type of tea, as some highly sensitive tea drinkers believe each type of tea imparts its own distinct seasoning to the pot.

"Every school girl, every school boy, knew how to make that exquisite pot of tea. You boiled the kettle, and just before it came to the boil, you half filled the teapot to warm it. When the kettle came to the boil, you kept it simmering while you threw out the water in the teapot and then put in a level spoonful of tea for each person and one for the pot. Up to four spoonfuls of tea from that sweetly odorous tea caddy would make the perfect pot. The caddy spoon was a special shape, like a

The one irrefutable requirement for the tea itself is that it be of the finest quality you can purchase. If you are new to buying tea, your local tea purveyor or gourmet shop should be able to assist you. Like most other Beacon Hill denizens of her day, Rose Nichols (and her parents before her) purchased their Hu-Kwa and other fine tea from Mark T. Wendell, now of West Concord, Massachusetts. Before moving to West Concord, the Mark Wendell Tea Company was owned and operated by Mark Wendell, a young Harvard graduate and resident of Beacon Hill. His tea became the favorite of the *Teacup Society* of Back Bay and Beacon Hill. He processed all the orders himself, packed the tea in his financial district office, and delivered it personally to the Nichols family residence at 55 Mount Vernon Street. The handsome one-pound tins, still in use today, can be viewed at the Nichols House Museum.

The Large Tea Party

For the sake of convenience, when preparing tea for a large group, you will find a piece of cheesecloth or muslin indispensable. As in Mary King's day, this item may be purchased from a hardware or cooking supply store, and may be used to make up your own large tea bags.

For a cozy tea with a few friends, the tea may be served in a simple china or clay pot. If, however, you are planning a tea for ten or more, a large silver or silver-plated tea urn, either borrowed or begged (if you do not have one in the family), should be used. In any case, it should be attractive, as it will sit in all its glory as the centerpiece of your tea table. The urn should be footed, allowing for a small candle (called a tea light) to be placed underneath it. When lit, this little flame will keep the tea hot throughout the party.

If you wish to stage a proper tea, you will also need, in addition to the tea urn, the implements of a traditional tea service, including a hot water pot, a creamer, and a sugar bowl. The purposes and proper uses of these items will be discussed in greater detail on the following pages.

The following method may be used for making a large quantity of tea in an urn: Before assembling your large tea bag, first measure your urn. Using the same cup that you will be using at your event, count out how many cups of water the tea urn will hold.

small silver shovel. You always . . . [took] the pot to the kettle, where you filled it, but never to the brim. You let it stand to 'draw' for three minutes.

"The tea had to be drunk out of china, as thin at the rim as you could afford. Otherwise you lost the taste of the tea. You put in milk sufficient to cloud the clear liquid, and sugar if you had a sweet tooth. Sugar or not was the only personal choice allowed. Everyone who came to the house was offered a cup of tea, as in Dostoyevsky. . . ."

Dame Muriel Sparks, remembering the precise tea ritual of her childhood, in *Curriculum Vitae*, 1992

If you are planning a formal tea party for 10 or more people, we encourage you to borrow or rent a tea urn, as even the largest teapots will require seemingly endless trips to the kitchen for refilling. If you live in a metropolitan area with antique shops, you might inquire about renting a tea service for the afternoon, and if required, teacups and saucers. (If you do succeed, be aware that one should never wash fine china in a dishwasher!) Or as an alternative, consider contacting a local caterer or party supplier to rent a large tea urn and any other service pieces that you will need. Another word of warning, however: Never use an urn that has previously contained coffee. The residue of the coffee will, without doubt, spoil the flavor of any tea.

That number will approximate the number of cups of tea you will be able to serve from the urn.

You will find that one large urn holding twenty cups will in fact produce almost double that amount of tea when you add the hot water and/or milk. As the party continues, the tea will become strengthened due to heat and evaporation. Be watchful, as you will continually need to fill the hot water pot, so that your pourer may dilute the strong tea on request.

Now it is time to cut prewashed cheesecloth or muslin into two pieces about five inches square. Place one square on top of another and spoon on loose tea leaves, measuring out one scant teaspoon per cup according to the urn's capacity. Tie up the cheesecloth bag loosely with a piece of butcher's string, leaving the tea leaves room to expand as the tea steeps. Note: one string needs to be long enough for the tea bag to be easily removed.

Most people will drink two cups of tea at a party; a generous rule of thumb would be to provide three cups per person. Make up an extra bag to have in reserve if needed. The teabags should be kept in an airtight container if you do not plan to use them soon after making them, as tea is fragile and quick to loose its flavor.

If your tea is set to begin at 3:30, start two kettles boiling at about 3:15 and simply keep them on low or simmer until it is time to steep the tea. The urn should now be in the kitchen awaiting your homemade tea bag. Place the tea bag inside the urn, being careful to leave the end of the butcher's string hanging over the side for easy removal. Pour the boiling water on top of the tea bag and allow it to steep for three to five minutes. (Note: We urge you to use only bottled or filtered water, which is free of the tainted, chlorinated taste of tap water.) Give the tea a good stir with a long-handled spoon. Should you have any doubt of its readiness, pour a little into a cup to taste before proceeding. If the tea is ready, the bag can then be removed and discarded, just as a spent tea bag would be removed from your teacup. At 3:30 the urn may be taken to the dining room and placed over a tea candle on a large silver tray in front of your esteemed pourer. When the pourer is seated and ready to serve—the tea party has commenced.

A silver water pot, similar in size and appearance to a regular silver teapot, should be part of your tea service. This footed water pot should be filled with hot water, and it too placed over a tea candle on the silver tray near your tea urn (see the diagram of the tea table on page 109).

Of course, Miss Rose had Mary to make all these preparations, but today you may be relying on a friend or two to keep hot water simmering, replenish empty dishes, remove used tea cups and saucers, and refresh the supply of milk and lemon. Your sharp eye is needed to keep all looking at its best.

Milk
You will need a silver pitcher of decent size (as not to need constant refilling), yet small enough to be convenient for pouring.

Yankee Ingenuity

While we tend to associate tea with the British Isles, it was in fact an American, Thomas Sullivan, who was credited with inventing the tea bag in 1908. Sullivan, a New York tea merchant, sent samples of tea to his clients in little silk pouches, with the intention that they would pour the contents into a teapot in the usual fashion. But, appreciating the new convenience, the recipients put the whole bag into the pot, and expected all future orders to arrive in this manner. When they did not, the customers complained to Sullivan, who recognized the great potential of the tea bag.

A Social History of Tea, by Jane Pettigrew

Mark T. Wendell, Importers of Fine Teas

When Elliot Johnson and his brother Alan bought the Mark T. Wendell Tea Company in 1971, an employee of Mr. Wendell related that in the early days, more often than not, the person who placed a tea order over the telephone had a decidedly Irish accent. The clerk, a Yankee trader by nature, began to encourage business by developing a Gaelic lilt of his own, and it was not long before he had engendered a confidentiality with his callers. Thus, he was never surprised to pick up the telephone and hear, "We'll have two pounds of the 'Cheericup' for the help (the cheapest grade of Ceylon tea available) and one pound of 'the poison' for the Master." Of course, the poison was Wendell's and Miss Nichols' cherished Hu-Kwa.

The debate continues not over milk versus cream; that argument has been long decided. Cream is too unctuous for tea—too overpowering. No, the argument is whether to use milk at all and, more importantly, when? If you are using your great grandmother's bone china, you should opt for pouring milk first into the cup; this will keep the very hot tea from doing damage to your heirloom.

Lemon

For some, the tea table would be incomplete without a dish of lemons, sliced in thin horizontal disks. Just as with milk, lemon is left to the individual's taste. It is felt by some that there are teas whose delicate flavor is enhanced with lemon and dampened by milk and vice versa. If, indeed, you have provided all the options you will meet everyone's requirements, and, of course, that is the aim of a good hostess.

Sugar

The sugar cube must have been invented for the tea table, and we suggest that you use it. It takes just one shaky hand attempting to transport a spoonful of sugar to make this point. So it is cubes and a nice set of tongs for the tea table.

Lacing the Tea

Without making any judgments about the intemperate habits of your guests, you may wish to be kind and add a decanter of good dark rum to the table. In some circles, although oddly not in Russia, this is known as a Russian tea.

The Proper Tea Sandwich

One of the most hopeless moments a hostess may encounter while giving a tea party is when she notices, while the event is in full swing, that her beautifully made tea sandwiches have begun to curl and dry up. In a matter of minutes, carefully assembled sandwiches have turned into cardboard that is quite capable of flight.

The following instructions will, we hope, help you to avoid this disaster: To make delicate tea sandwiches, plan on using thin bread (sometimes called diet thin). The freshness of the bread is very important—it should feel soft and springy. If a slice seems thick try using a rolling pin with (or without) a cotton sleeve and "iron" it gently by rolling it in one direction. Try to work with spreads that can be softened, such as cream cheese, butter, or mayonnaise, because they are kinder to the soft bread. Spread softened butter or mayonnaise on the inside half of the top and bottom bread slices. This helps to keep the sandwiches moist. Sandwiches should be made the same day they are to be served, but allow time for them to "cure." To save time during assembly, cut crusts off the bread in stacks. Using a good serrated knife, you can easily trim eight to ten slices of bread at one time—just be sure to cut the bread slices squarely so you will not have a problem "matching" slices when you assemble.

Hu-Kwa

Many people wonder about the difference between China's Hu-Kwa and Lapsang Souchong teas. Hu-Kwa, the milder of the two, is smoked over pine needles. Lapsang Souchong is smoked over the more pungent wood of the camphor tree. The name Hu-Kwa was used by Mr. Wendell in honor of Houqua, the famous Chinese tea merchant with whom Wendell's uncle, the original owner and importer, had traded in the early nineteenth century.

To Order Tea

While no longer personally
delivered by Mark T. Wendell,
his many wonderful teas, in tins
of the same original design, are
still available by mail order as
well as at his shop in West
Concord, Massachusetts.

To receive information and an
order form, write to the company at 50 Beharrell Street,
P.O. Box 1312, West Concord,
Massachusetts 01742,
telephone 978-369-3709,
or fax 978-369-7972.
To order on line, visit
www. Marktwendell.com

Gourmet teas may also be
found at Cardullo's Gourmet
Shoppe, 6 Brattle Street,
Cambridge, Massachusetts;
telephone 617-491-8888. This
family-run business is an old-
time favorite for fine tea and
other difficult-to-locate imported items.

New on the scene, Tealuxe tea
rooms in Boston and Cambridge
offer fine imported tea. Telephone 508-520-7887 or visit
www.tealuxe.com

It is best to store sandwiches in a row in a rectangular pan, cover-
ing them with a fresh dishcloth that has been run under cold
water and then completely wrung out, and then refrigerating
them for several hours. If you layer the sandwiches, a lightly
dampened paper towels between the layers keeps them moist and
can sharpen flavor. You can bring them back to room temperature,
but do not leave them uncovered; the bread will become stale.
You can use fancy cookie cutters to make various shaped sandwiches, but a small triangle or rectangle is the tradition.

Setting the Tea Table

A tea for twenty-five or more will need a large table, a minimum of eight feet long and four feet wide. This will allow for the option of two pourers, one at each end, and allow you to serve two different teas with plenty of room for both food and implements. The diagram on page 109 is an example of how a tea table might be set out. An easy flow of people, not a long line or a crush, is the aim.

A dish of sliced lemons with a small fork for serving, and dainty spoons and forks are ideal—not your large dinner flatware, *please*. Small dessert plates should be used and may be stacked one upon the other. If you can provide linen cocktail napkins, all the better, but good quality paper napkins may also be used. To save space on the table, you can pre-stack the napkins onto the dessert plates. Prior to serving, cut all food into dainty portions as not to upset the table by having individuals slice and cut up the food *in situ*. Similarly, if you serve cake, make thin slices.

"I hear the shadow of one old lady saying to me, 'and never biscuits out of a tin, my dear.'"

The Constance Spry Cookery Book, 1957

Butter Curls

The good hostess will take extraordinary measures to ensure a presentable tea table. Consider, for instance, the advice on curling butter offered by *Beeton's Book of Household Management*: "Tie a strong cloth by two of the corners to an iron hook in the wall; make a knot with the other ends, so that a stick might pass through. Put the butter in the cloth; twist it tightly over a dish, into which the butter will fall through the knot, so forming small and pretty light strings." Happily a better result may be achieved by simply purchasing a "butter curler" at your local kitchen supply store.

Each pourer's setting should be identical and so, too, should the tea food being served, thus avoiding the problem of a guest spotting a favorite item on the opposite side of the table and being unable to reach it.

A crisp, starched white linen tablecloth is traditional, but if you avoid "the riot of color" look, which would detract from your food, a plain, light color linen cloth will do.

A floral centerpiece is always appropriate, as are candles, which reflect off silver and china to impart a warm glow to your table. Some say that it is funereal to use lit candles before nightfall, but it is our sentiment that candlelight beginning at dusk on a chilly winter day can add a good deal of cheer to a room.

A Formal Tea Table

Cups & Saucers
Cups & Saucers
Cups & Saucers

A Cup & Saucer

Hot Water   Milk

Tea Urn

Dish of Sliced Lemon
Sugar Bowl & Tongs
Teaspoons
Small Forks
Napkins
Dessert Plates

Lace Cookies

Rum Cakes

Tea Sandwiches

Orange Chiffon Cake

Candied Peel

Spinach Squares

Ham & Cheese Puffs

Candles

Sliced Fruitcake

Candied Peel

Orange Chiffon Cake

Floral
Centerpiece
&
Decorations

Candies

Tea Sandwiches

Sliced Fruitcake

Candles

Ham & Cheese Puffs

Spinach Squares

Rum Cakes

Lace Cookies

Dessert Plates
Napkins
Small Forks
Teaspoons
Sugar Bowl & Tongs
Dish of Sliced Lemon

Tea Urn

Hot Water   Milk

A Cup & Saucer

Cups & Saucers
Cups & Saucers
Cups & Saucers

At a large, formal tea it is considerate to offer your guests small tables with chairs. This is a necessity if you are serving more than finger foods.

Notes for the Cook

A few basic rules for successful cookies, squares, and cakes

Before you begin, read each recipe all the way through—twice if you think necessary.

Use only the freshest and best quality ingredients.

For quick and easy assembling, gather all ingredients in pre-measured amounts.

Bring ingredients to near room temperature—even eggs should have the chill off; ingredients blend better when not frigid.

Use only U.S. Graded Large eggs, as they are the only egg reliably uniform in size.

Always use unsalted butter—salt may be added but never subtracted.

Unless indicated otherwise, the flour is white, all-purpose.

Always preheat oven prior to use.

If you are making several batches of cookies or cakes, have extra identical cookie sheets or pans at hand, or allow the pans to cool between batches to keep heat uniform and consistent.

Closely watch cookies, particularly thin cookies, for the telltale signs of readiness indicated in the recipes.

Leave adequate space between lace cookie varieties; they will spread out.

Cooling Cookies

When cookies are deemed ready, immediately remove the pan from the oven. Using a thin-bladed spatula, quickly test to see if cookies are firm enough and cool enough to be removed easily. If so, continue the process of removing and setting the cookies onto racks to finish cooling. With some cookies (lace cookies, for example), it is important to act quickly, so be prepared. If cookies stick, returning the pan to the hot oven for a minute or two may make them more pliable. Cool completely on racks before storing.

Cooling Squares

If you intend to use the squares immediately, they may be cut in the pan when partially cooled. Use a large, sharp-bladed knife to make neat squares or rectangles. They may then be left in the pan until completely cooled. If you are not going to use the squares straight away or are planning to freeze them, do not cut them into pieces at this time—refrigerate or freeze them whole. When the time comes to serve the squares, partially thaw and cut into small squares or rectangles by using a large, sharp knife. Always trim and neaten the edges.

Storing Cookies and Squares

It is important to emphasize that cookies and squares should always be thoroughly cooled before storing—warm cookies will produce steam and become soft. Store each variety of cookies and squares separately. If packed in airtight containers—plastic, tin, or sealed plastic bags—cookies or squares will retain their freshness for two weeks, and sometimes longer. We successfully stored the Swedish wafers for one month in an airtight tin. Most cookies and squares will store in the freezer for three months.

Baking Cakes

The cake recipes we offer are of the sponge, chiffon, and butter varieties. The following basic rules and techniques should be read and considered:

When constructing a cake, carefully follow the order in which the ingredients are listed, as the result may vary drastically if you do not.

Sturdy pans of medium-weight aluminum are best for baking cakes.

For greasing cake pans, use a good vegetable shortening either in solid form or spray, rather than margarine or butter.

Unless the recipe says so, do not grease pans for chiffon and sponge cakes. For proper rising, these cakes need clean sides to climb.

Most other types of cake recipes need greased baking pans, and some call for greased and dusted with flour. *To dust with flour:* place a tablespoon of flour into greased pan and shake and tap on the kitchen counter, turning the pan to insure a light dusting of flour coats the entire pan. Discard excess flour.

All Teas Are Not Tea

The French are precise in distinguishing the names given to hot beverages. Besides thé, they steep infusions and tisanes. We, on the other hand, call almost any warm drink tea—be it peach, orange, or beef.

As a rule, loaf, bundt, and tube pans are greased and dusted with flour.

When directions call for lining a cake pan, we suggest you use waxed paper, although some cooks prefer parchment paper (available at cooking supply stores). *To line a cake pan:* you will need to line the bottom only. Use a piece of waxed paper that is slightly larger than the base of the cake pan. Place the cake pan on waxed paper, and trace around the outside edge with a pencil or pen. Cut just inside the line you have traced, and fit the round into the bottom of the pan. If it is too large, trim off a little paper, to fit neatly into the pan. *To line a loaf pan:* line the bottom and sides only, *not* the ends. For example, if you line a 8" x 4" x 3" loaf pan, you will need to cut a piece of waxed paper that is 8" x 10". (The length of the pan, which is 8", will determine one measurement. The other measurement is simply the combined total of the width of the pan, which is 4", and its two sides which are each 3".) Fit the waxed paper into the bottom of the pan and trim where necessary. It is all right if the paper extends beyond the top of the sides of the pan as the extra is sometimes useful in removing the cake from the pan.

Loaf and tube pans should be filled no more than two-thirds or three-quarters full with cake batter.

The general rule for baking is that small cakes are baked in the top half of the oven at approximately 375° F, while large cakes are

No Chocolate?

The strong, rich flavor of chocolate is not the traditional companion to the delicate flavor of fine tea. Hence, we found no recipes in Mary King's file that made use of chocolate as an ingredient—perhaps chocolate connoted a certain decadence that was not suitable to afternoon tea, and its often moist and messy nature might have compromised the tidy, bite-size offerings of the tea table.

baked in the middle or bottom half of the oven at a preheated temperature of approximately 375° F, then reduced to 350° F.

Cool cakes thoroughly on wire racks before storing. To determine if the cake is done, gently press on the surface; the cake should spring back without leaving a dent. Another good method to test for doneness is to insert a wooden skewer into the center of the cake. If it comes out clean of any batter, the cake is ready to be removed from the oven.

Cooling and Storing Cakes or Mini-cakes

Most cakes, other than cream cakes, should be stored at room temperature. Tightly covered in plastic wrap (the kind that is specified for freezer use) or stored in tightly sealed plastic bags, most cakes should stay fresh for four to five days.

Please note, however, that if you wish to keep a crusty surface, you should not store the cake in plastic, but instead loosely cover with aluminum foil.

Most cakes freeze well and for long periods of time—up to six months. *To thaw*: unwrap to keep the moisture accumulated while it was freezing away from the cake.

Soaking a Cake with Rum

If you would like to particularly please the men among your tea-party guests, soak any rich cake with rum or brandy while it is still warm by piercing a wooden skewer down through the cake a dozen times and spooning ¼ cup of the liqueur of your choice over the top.

Ad finem

"Hospitality is a most excellent virtue; but care must be taken that the love of company, for its own sake, does not become a prevailing passion; for then the habit is no longer hospitality, but dissipation. Reality and truthfulness in this . . . are the points to be studied; for, as Washington Irving well says, 'There is an emanation from the heart in genuine hospitality, which cannot be described, but is immediately felt, and puts the stranger at once at his ease.'"

—Beeton's Book of Household Management

How I Went Out to Service

by Louisa May Alcott

Devotees of Little Women *may be surprised to learn that Bostonian Louisa May Alcott, at age 18 and from a genteel but financially disadvantaged family, briefly joined the ranks of "women in service" (see pages 60-61) as a domestic in the home of an insufferable "Mr. R." and his delicate sister. Her adventure recounted in an abbreviated version, began auspiciously enough:*

I do housework at home for love; why not do it abroad for money?

My sisters laughed when they heard the new plan, [and] the highly respectable relatives held up their hands in holy horror at the idea of leaving the paternal roof to wash other people's teacups, nurse other people's ails, and obey other people's orders for hire. . . . If doing work hurts my respectability, I wouldn't give much for it. My aristocratic ancestors don't feed or clothe me and my democratic ideas of honesty and honor won't let me be idle or dependent.

I got ready my small wardrobe, consisting of two calico dresses and one delaine, made by myself, also some uncompromising blue aprons and three tidy little sweeping caps; for I had some English notions about housework and felt that my muslin hair-protectors would be useful in some of the "light labors" I was to undertake. It is needless to say they were very becoming. Then firmly embracing my family, I set forth, one cold January day, with my little trunk, a stout heart, and a five-dollar bill for my fortune.

I arrived at twilight. . . . Peering in at an open door. . . . Old portraits stared at me from the walls and a damp chill froze the marrow in my bones. [The next morning] I fell to work with a will, eager . . . to put things to right, for many hard jobs had evidently been waiting for a stronger arm. . . . [I] soon found that my hands would be kept busy with the realms of [Mr. R.], who . . . needed cosseting with dainty food, hot fires, soft beds, and endless service.

Gradually all the work of the house had been slipped into my hands. . . . I bore it as long as I could, and then freed my mind in a declaration of independence, delivered in the kitchen, where he found me scrubbing the hearth. . . . Having made up my mind to go before the month was out, I said nothing, but dug paths, brought water from the well, split kindling, and sifted ashes.

After suffering the ultimate humiliation of being told to clean Mr. R.'s boots—not just a pair, but a whole shed full—Louisa left her "fellow inmates" on a bleak March afternoon.

Behind me stood the dull old house; before me rumbled the wheelbarrow bearing my dilapidated wardrobe; and in my pocket reposed what I fondly hoped was if not a liberal, at least an honest return for seven weeks of the hardest work I ever did.

Unable to resist the desire to see what my earnings were, I opened the purse and beheld four dollars. I looked from my poor chapped grimy, chilblained hands to the paltry sum that was considered reward for all the hard labor they had done. . . .

My experiment seemed a dire failure and I mourned it as such for years; but more than once in my life I have been grateful for that serio-comico experience, since it has taught me many lessons. One of the most useful of these has been the power of successfully making a companion, not a servant, of those whose aid I need, and helping to gild their honest wages with the sympathy and justice which can sweeten the humblest and lighten the hardest task.

Notes

To the Reader
The Constance Spry Cookery Book, by Constance Spry and Rosemary Hume, J.M. Dent and Sons, Ltd., 1957.

Preface
Page v, the Teacup Society; the name given to the genteel residents of Victorian Boston, *Main Currents of American Thought*, V.L. Parrington, Harcourt Brace and Co., 1930.
Page vi, "The Mothers of Conservation," by John H. Mitchell, *The Sanctuary, The Journal of the Massachusetts Audubon Society*, Jan./Feb., 1996.

Part One: Rose Standish Nichols
Page 2, A conversation with William and Joan Shurcliff, Cambridge, 1999.
Page 2, *Beacon Hill: Hub of the Universe*, by Frances Minturn Howard, Yankee, Inc. 1977.
Page 2, "Mary King: Keeper of Tradition," by Elizabeth W. Driscoll, 1982.
Page 3, A conversation with Polly Thayer Starr, March 1, 2000.
Page 4, Frances Minturn Howard, *Beacon Hill: Hub of the Universe*.
Page 4, A conversation with William and Joan Shurcliff, Cambridge, 1999.
Page 5, *Some Descendents of Richard Nichols of Ipswich*, compiled and written by Arthur Howard Nichols, from the New England Historic Genealogical Society, call number SGNIC.
Page 8, *Lively Days: Some Memoirs of Margaret Homer Shurcliff*, by Margaret Homer Shurcliff (nee Nichols), Taipei Literature House, Ltd., 1965.
Pages 8-11, *Footprints of the Past: Images of Cornish, New Hampshire & The Cornish Colony*, by Virginia Reed Colby and James B. Atkinson, New Hampshire Historial Society, 1966.
Pages 9-10, Frances Duncan quote, "A Cornish Garden," *Country Life in America*, March 1908.
Pages 13-14, Rose Nichols letters, Schlesinger Library, Radcliffe Institute for Advanced Studies.
Pages 14, 15, 17, Conversations with Joan Shurcliff, Cambridge, 1999.
Page 15, A conversation with Polly Thayer Starr, March 1, 2000.
Page 17, *Rose Standish Nichols As We Knew Her: A Tribute to a Friend*, by Friends of Rose Standish Nichols, c. 1986.
Pages 17-18, Correspondence, Rose Nichols writing to her sister Marian, Schlesinger Library, Radcliffe Institute for Advanced Studies.

Part Two: Recipes & Reminiscences

Page 24, "Mary King: Keeper of Tradition," by Elizabeth W. Driscoll, 1982.

Page 25, *Beacon Hill: Hub of the Universe*, by Frances Minturn Howard.

Pages 27, 29, Correspondence, Elizabeth Nichols to her daughters Rose and Marian, 1893, Schlesinger Library, Radcliffe Institute for Advanced Studies.

Page 29, *The Nature of Massachusetts*, Addison-Wesley, 1996.

Page 36, Dr. Howard Nichols letter, 1894, Schlesinger Library, Radcliffe Institute for Advanced Studies.

Page 38, "It was hardly love at first sight of Huggins Farm," from *The Reminiscences of Augustus Saint-Gaudens*, edited and amplified by Homer Saint-Gaudens, Century Company, 1913.

Page 41, *Footprints in the Past: Images of Cornish, New Hampshire & The Cornish Colony*, by Virgina Reed Colby and James B. Atkinson.

Page 42, Herbert Adams, *Footprints of the Past: Images of Cornish, New Hampshire*, by Virginia Reed Colby and James B. Atkinson.

Page 45, *Yankee*, September 1991.

Pages 48, 53, *Spanish and Portuguese Gardens*, by Rose Standish Nichols, Houghton Mifflin, 1924.

Page 50, Letter, Willa Sibert Cather, May, 7, 1908, Collection of the Nichols House Museum.

Page 54, Letter, Rose Nichols to her sister Marian, May 30, 1900, Schlesinger Library, Radcliffe Institute for Advanced Studies.

Page 54, The Wyndham Sisters, in the collection of New York's Metropolitan Museum, painted by John Singer Sargent in 1899.

Page 55, Asher Wertheimer, prominent art patron and friend of Sargent; portrait in the collection of Tate Britain, London, painted in 1898.

Page 56, The French critic Paul Bion in *The Reminiscences of Augustus Saint-Gaudens*, edited and amplified by Homer Saint-Gaudens.

Pages 60-61, "Mary King: Keeper of Tradition," by Elizabeth Driscoll.

Page 60, General research from *Daughters of Erin*, by Hasia Dinar, Johns Hopkins Press, 1983.

Page 61, "How I Went Out to Service," Louisa May Alcott, an article from *The Independent*, Vol. XXVI, No. 1331, June 4, 1874, Orchard House.

Page 64, "Mary King: Keeper of Traditions," by Elizabeth Driscoll, 1982.

Page 65, *The Boston Athenaeum: A Reader's Guide*, by Ann Wadsworth, E.H. Roberts Co., 1995.

Pages 74-75, *The Boston Cooking School Cookbook*, by Fannie Merritt Farmer, Sixth Edition, Little Brown and Co., 1939.

Page 75, *The Book of Boston, The Victorian Period*, by Marjorie Drake Ross, Hastings House, 1964.

Page 76, Letter, Augustus Saint-Gaudens to Rose Nichols, undated, Special Collections, Dartmouth College Library, Dartmouth, NH.

Page 77, Conversation with William H. Pear II, curator, Nichols House Museum, February 1999.

Page 78, *The Constance Spry Cookery Book*, by Constance Spry and Rosemary Hume.

Page 80, *Lively Days*, by Margaret Homer Shurcliff.

Page 82, *The Book of Boston, The Victorian Period*, by Marjorie Drake Ross, Hastings House.

Pages 85-87, "Arthur Nichols: A Passion for Bells," by Jessie Ravage, in *The Clapper, The Official Journal of the North American Guild of Change Ringers*, Vol. 16, No. 2, Spring 1989.

Page 90, Letter, Elizabeth Nichols to her daughter Rose, December 19, 1893, Schlesinger Library, Radcliffe Institute for Advanced Studies.

Page 92, *Beeton's Book of Household Management*, A First Edition Facsimile, by Isabella Beeton, Farrar, Straus and Giroux, 1969.

Page 98, *The Constance Spry Cookery Book*, by Constance Spry and Rosemary Hume.

Part Three: Planning and Preparing a Tea Party

Page 100-101, *Curriculum Vitae*, by Dame Muriel Sparks, Houghton Mifflin, 1992.

Page 103, *A Social History of Tea*, by Jane Pettigrew, National Trust Enterprises, Ltd., 2001.

Pages 104-105, Conversations with Elliot Johnson, proprietor of The Mark T. Wendell Tea Company, 2001.

Page 112, *Curriculum Vitae*, by Dame Muriel Sparks.

Ad finem

Pages 117-118, "How I Went Out to Service," an article from *The Independent*, Vol. XXVI, No. 1331, June 4, 1874, Orchard House.

Illustrations

Page x, Photograph, Rose Nichols by George Taloumis, August 1953.

Page 6, Photograph, Augustus Saint-Gaudens and family, tea at Aspet in Cornish, c. 1898, courtesy of the State Library of Massachusetts Special Collections.

Page 12, Photograph, Marian and Rose Nichols with a friend in Salzburg, 1894, Nichols House Museum Collection.

Page 16, Photograph, Boston hats: the sewing circle at 55 Mount Vernon Street, c. 1950, Nichols House Museum Collection.

Page 24, Illustration of a tea urn, by Elaine Negroponte.

Page 49, Illustration of Roman Emperor Hadrian's villa at Tivoli, by Rose Standish Nichols in *Italian Pleasure Gardens*, Dodd, Mead & Co., 1931.

Page 61, Illustration of the Nichols House tea service, by Paul Leahy.

Page 69, Illustration of the Nichols House staircase, by Paul Leahy.

Page 77, Illustration of Rose Nichols' bedroom, by Paul Leahy.

Pages 122-123, *A Suggested Tour* map, by Fritz Westman.

A Suggested Tour

This tour will take approximately 60 minutes to walk at a leisurely pace. If you wish to tour either the Boston Athenaeum or Nichols House Museum, call ahead for hours, and leave extra time.

We suggest you begin the tour at the Boston Athenaeum (far right) at the crest of Beacon Hill and end at the Boston Public Library at Copley Square.

Do consider exploring the shops and sights along the way—and ending the tour with a refreshing cup of tea at one of the Back Bay cafés.

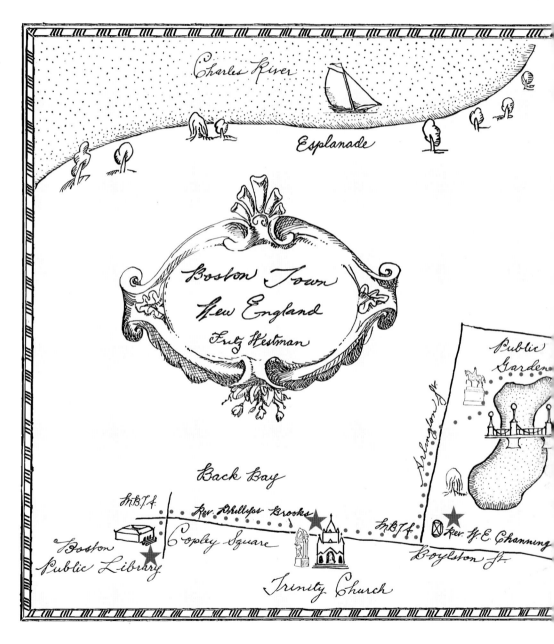

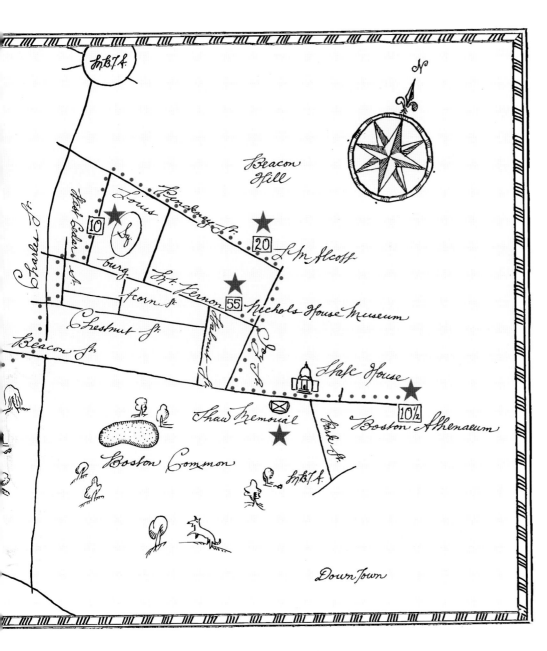

★ **Boston Athenaeum, 1807**
10½ Beacon Street
(Call 617-277-0270 for
tours and hours.)
www.bostonathenaeum.org

★ **Saint-Gaudens Memorial
to Civil War hero Robert
Gould Shaw and the 54th
Regiment, 1897**
across from the Massa-
chusetts State House

★ **Nichols House Museum,
1804 (home to the Nichols
family from 1885)**
55 Mount Vernon Street
(Call 617-227-6993 for
tours and hours.)

★ **House where Louisa May
Alcott's family rented rooms**
20 Pinckney Street

★ **Alcott's residence at the
time of her death in 1888**
10 Louisburg Square

★ **Bronze of minister
and abolitionist William
Ellery Channing, 1903**
at the corner of the Boston
Public Garden, facing
Arlington Street.

★ **Statue of the Reverend
Phillips Brooks, 1907**
on the Boylston Street side
of Trinity Church.

★ **Boston Public Library
at Copley Square, 1895**
(Call 617-536-5400 for
free tours and hours.)
www.bpl.org